Midnight
in New
England

Midnight in New England

Tales of the Strange and Mysterious

by SCOTT THOMAS

Cover photograph © Gerolf Kalt/zefa/Corbis
Interior illustration by Christopher Cart

ISBN: 978-0-89272-732-2

Printed at Versa Press, East Peoria, Illinois

5   4   3   2   1

Down East Books
Camden, Maine
A division of Down East Enterprise
Book orders: 800-685-7962
www.downeastbooks.com
Distributed to the trade by National Book Network

Library of Congress Catalog-in-Publication Data:

Thomas, Scott, 1959-
  Midnight in New England : strange and mysterious tales / by Scott Thomas.
      p. cm.
   ISBN-13: 978-0-89272-732-2 (trade pbk. : alk. paper)
   1. Supernatural--Fiction. 2. New England--Fiction. 3. Horror tales. 4. Fantasy
fiction. I. Title.
   PS3620.H6423M53 2007
   813'.6--dc22
                                        2007019396

For Peggy

Contents

The Dead of Midwinter

It was shortly before the time of Victoria and winter had come to our small New England village. Winter, unlike so many traveling merchants who failed to notice the place, knew just where to find us.

There was white on the fields and flat against the roofs and nesting in the crooks of trees; it smothered the pond where ice had prepared a surface.

It was harsh and cold that December, as I recall it, and one was made to understand why so many creatures hibernated. The temperature had a personality all its own, fumbling about our homes like great invisible hands determined to find flaws through which to usher drafts.

The drafts themselves were like a disease that stole into the blood where (reversing their polarity) they spawned fevers, as if to mock us, as if to say, *here is the warmth you dearly miss.* But it was not the spring's soft warmth, nor even the summer's swelter that burned under the flesh.

The snow was blue with moonlight when our neighbor Caleb Wightman woke from his dream. The midnight church banged like a wagon full of kettles, its noise spreading over and falling upon the houses like heavy snow.

Unsettled by his dreaming, Caleb lit a candle and sat shuddering in his bed. Despite the bitter air, his nightshirt was damp against his skinny frame and the candle's glow made the drops of sweat on his brow glint like the heads of copper nails.

Caleb was an old widower, his beloved Hannah now six months in the churchyard; so he attributed her voice to the wind, or a remnant of his dream. Too cold and unsteady to bring himself to abandon his covers long enough to re-light the fire, he opted to remain sitting there, half-cocooned.

New England's wintry wind was a unique musical instrument capable of a wide range of sounds. Shaping itself to the hills, or stealing through the birches, it might hiss like a sleigh, or roar like the sea, or brush against a house like a cat. Caleb had never heard it sing until that night.

The wind knew his name, it seemed, but it was not the wind, he determined at length. It was the voice of his wife.

In the middle of the snowy night, I was awakened by a small hand that found my foot through the blankets. Lifting my head, I looked to see the pale, disheveled figure of my young Patty.

"Father," she said, "Mr. Wightman is out dancing in the snow. He's unclothed."

I chuckled, and rising to return the child to her bed, assured her that she had merely been dreaming. I tucked the covers up about her throat.

"Listen," Patty said, "he is singing."

"The wind and nothing more," I insisted gently, stroking her head.

The girl seemed to have a slight fever, I found. I told this to her mother when I returned to my own chamber. We would need to mind her closely, as the village had lost a number of its residents in the preceding weeks. Fever was a devious thing—a killing heat in the year's deep cold.

Settling back into my mattress, I heard the breeze rattling the windows, a mist of flakes now sighing through the surrounding wood. It hissed like the kegs of cider fermenting in the cellar.

"That's curious," I noted in the morning, pulling the curtain aside to see what the clouds had brought us.

"What's curious?" my Wilmot asked.

"There appear to be tracks in the snow."

She peered over my shoulder. Tracks were not uncommon—often we woke to find evidence of deer and smaller beasts.

"Good heavens," Wilmot said, a hand against her bosom. "Whoever would go barefoot in such weather?"

I dressed myself and headed out, snug in great coat and hat and gloves. While snow continued to accumulate, as if to hide the imprints, I saw that they did indeed seem to come from a human's naked foot. I followed them.

The trail meandered erratically, but eventually brought me to the whitened road, then westward toward the edge of the village. Tree and reed and bush were softened in their white dressing, and the far hills scarcely showed for the innumerable layers of falling flakes.

The longer I followed the tracks, the more I was made conscious of the words my Patty had spoken the night before. Perhaps poor old Mr. Wightman had fallen prey to some form of lunacy. He had been troubled with grief since the loss of his Hannah.

Sure enough, the trail led to the Wightman house, a sad thing sitting there in the cold, though the stark, contorted maples around it were soothed by the snow. No smoke issued from the large central chimney.

I trudged to the door and rapped with my stick. I waited, blinking in the snow, but no answer came. I knocked again, louder this time, and called out a hullo.

At length I tried the door and found it unbolted. It was chill and tenebrous inside and the smell of wood smoke was only a memory from charred log remnants in the keeping room.

"Hullo, Caleb," I called into the still house, where my inquiry dissipated without reciprocation.

I made my way up the stairs and to my neighbor's bedchamber. The cold was sharpest in that room. Even so, Caleb Wightman was sprawled without garments on his bed, free even of his bedcovers. He was a ghastly sight to see, bony and blue and staring up into the netting of his bed canopy. He was cold to the touch, having been dead for some hours.

I noticed the window to the right of the paneled fireplace wall was open and a dusting of snow had lighted on the sill. Shivering, I turned to close this when from behind me, from the direction of the bed, I heard a soft voice wheeze . . .

"She kissed me."

The window banged down and I spun to regard the figure on the bed. It appeared as if he was smiling.

After summoning the undertaker, the reverend, and the sheriff, I made my way home through the cold. The church bells rang noon, their repetitions muffled by the relentless snowfall.

A friendly, if ghostly, chain of smoke was drifting up from the chimney of my house and I stomped my boots on the stoop to loosen the snow. Welcome warmth greeted me in the kitchen, though there was woe in my young wife's eye.

"Something is the matter, my dear?" I asked.

"Patty is not well, I fear. Her fever worsens by the hour." She wrung her small hands and added, "She imagines strange things . . . "

Without bothering to remove my coat, I thumped up the stairs and then stepped softly into my daughter's room. She looked so very small there on the bed, her meager bulk only slightly mounding the covers, the mound rising weakly with her breath. Her eyes were closed and there was sweat on her forehead, like beads of gilted ice in the fire-glow.

Though I meant to be quiet, Patty stirred. Her eyes opened and she wheezed.

"*He kissed me,*" she said with a smile.

Herrick's Inn

Sudbury, Massachusetts, 1757

Spring had come to the woods behind the inn—the evidence was both subtle and grand. Fiddleheads poked up from the damp, dark earth at the edge of the pond, like the unfurling tails of tiny submerged dragons. Flowering trees stood in the midst of their bare gray counterparts, radiant bonnets of pink in the lowering evening light. Breezes rustled the dry brown carpet of leaves that winter had left behind, as dusk brought a coolness that might have passed for September. But this was the first of May, and lovers met in the quiet spring wood.

Rebecca Herrick was the innkeeper's only surviving daughter. The other three had perished ten years previous when Rebecca was young. Consumption had come reaping. Now, at eighteen, she was her father's prize, and was it any wonder? She was an angelic creature, her hair an amber spill framing the round pallor of her face. Her features were fine and her figure appealingly plump. Her father did his best to keep her in the kitchen, safely away from the eyes of the lonely travelers who frequented the inn.

But her father had failed to keep John Easty from noticing the girl. The young doctor's apprentice, who had been visiting an ill brother in Grafton, was on his way back to Boston when he stopped at Herrick's Inn. It was December dusk and a sluggish snow had fallen on the round New England hills, had whispered into the gray woods. The old inn had been a welcome sight, its windows warm and golden. The innkeep's daughter had been a welcome sight as well.

Warming by the fire, John had watched as the girl went about her duties in the tavern room. She was graceful and sweet and her laughter had a lilting quality as it rose up into the dark beams above.

Subsequent visits to Herrick's Inn followed, and John courted Rebecca, unbeknownst to her father. At first they met in the woods behind the inn, but later John climbed a tree by the inn and stole into her bedchamber. They spent several nights together over the following months.

Now, under the cool, darkening May sky, the lovers embraced within their shelter of trees, a tethered horse nearby. John could smell the kitchen smoke in Rebecca's hair as he pressed her to his chest. Her belly was against his, soft and warm—not the hard, pouting thing it had been during his last visit.

Rebecca's parents had never noticed that she had been carrying a child. Her plumpness, apron, and the full skirts common to the day had kept the fact secret.

"It was dead at birth," Rebecca said in a whisper.

"Oh, dear," John groaned, holding her tighter.

"Not to worry, I buried him in a lovely spot and said prayers."

"A boy?"

Rebecca nodded against him. She felt him shiver and said, "Please do not fret. It is really for the best. Father would have done away with me, if ever he knew."

John agreed quietly.

Rebecca pulled back and looked up. She gave him a fetching smile and touched his cheek. "We are together, nothing matters so much as that."

John took her hand and kissed it. "Yes. That *is* what matters."

They moved slowly toward the inn and its outbuildings. The windowless icehouse was a dark shape in the gloom. Geese flew honking over a willow and a breeze rattled the leafy carpet.

"You must wait until you see my parents' window go dark," Rebecca reminded the man. "My window shall be unlocked."

"Unlocked, yes, of course—I shouldn't want to break it," he joked.

Rebecca squeezed his hand. "I've missed you so," she said, and then headed off across the small grassy field that separated the woods from the back of the inn.

When the last of the laughter had died away in the tavern and the last guest had staggered up to his room, Rebecca hurried to sweep the floor and wipe the ale-scented tables. Her hair, loosened from under her bonnet by the steam in the kitchen, hung in her face.

She straightened the chairs and made certain that the logs were safely positioned in the hearth before taking up a candle and climbing the stairs to her room. The inn was quiet at this late hour, but for some muffled snoring, heard as she passed the guest rooms.

In her chamber, she set the candle down by the bed and quickly, though cautiously, unlocked and partly opened her window. She had taken to keeping it shut in all weather, ever since the strange noises had begun coming from the woods some weeks back.

Rebecca removed her bonnet, combed out her long hair and pinched her cheeks to give them color. She heard sounds coming from outside, someone moving slowly up the great old maple that grew close to the inn. Smiling, she removed her garments and tossed them aside, unceremoniously. The air gave her a chill. She slid into bed, pulling the covers to her throat, resting her head back on the pillow she had used to smother the baby.

While the candle was largely burnt down, the wick could have used a trimming, and the flame burned too high. The glare on the glass prevented her from making out the vague figure that was now pushing open the window.

John stood in the dark wood, stomping in place to keep warm, as one by one the windows in the distant inn went dark. The chill made him restless, made him imagine the heat of Rebecca's body.

The leaves rattled somewhere, and once he turned and thought that he saw a small hunched animal duck behind a tree—a skunk or a raccoon, likely. Animals sounded in the dim expanse of tangled trees. Living in the city, he had grown unaccustomed to the sounds of wildlife, had forgotten how some birds could sound like a baby crying.

Another window went dark—the window that belonged to the innkeeper and his wife. Grinning, John stepped out from the edge of the wood, into the small field.

A light glowed in Rebecca's room. He had reached the inn, old and somber looking, rambling—the ancient structure added to over the years, grown out from its original humble size. There were several scraggly lilac bushes along the base of the structure, their purple flowers just days from blooming. The stately maple loomed, reached up past Rebecca's open window, towered over the roof.

John grunted as he hefted himself into the lower branches. There were a good many sturdy limbs to climb on—no worse than a ladder. The window was close, he could see the candlelight wavering on the ceiling of the room. He heard something as well, but could not readily identify the sound. *Was it slurping?*

Successful at last, John gripped the edge of the open window and pulled himself up. He looked in at the bed, at Rebecca dead and naked upon it, with a small gray form crouched on her belly. Its hairless head was round, and it stopped nursing at a pale breast to turn and glare at him. It hissed.

Somehow John managed not to scream. He scrambled awkwardly down the tree and fell several feet from the bottom. He ran to where his horse was tethered, just inside the dark wood, and spurred it swiftly to the road.

His heartbeat matched the pounding of the hooves, as the mare galloped along the track. Even when John closed his eyes he could see the baby's face, like a small rotting pumpkin, the disintegrating flesh lit softly, internally, as if by a chunk of the moon. Mostly he saw the eyes—darker than a skull's, darker than the night into which his horse carried him.

Laben Blois's Death

Laben Blois had a farm just north of Barnstable. His overworked plow horse, who Laben's children called Old Maggie, but he just called "damn lazy nag," died one winter's night when the barn caught fire. Without a horse, Laben didn't know how he would run his farm. He had suffered a poor harvest the previous year and could not afford to buy another horse. Laben, however, knew of an old Indian man in a cabin in a valley three miles to the south. Laben's children called the man Buck.

Buck kept mostly to himself, though he traded animal furs with the local villagers on occasion.

Laben knew that Buck had a beautiful auburn mare. He decided that he could make better use of the beast than the old Indian could.

So, Laben crept off one night after his wife and children had gone to sleep. He walked on dirt paths until he reached the cabin where old Buck lived. It was a still moonless night. Laben leaned on his rifle, outside, waiting. The old Indian was still awake, for an amber light filled the cabin's windows.

Laben moved for the door, but it opened just as he reached for the latch. Old Buck stood silhouetted in the doorway. Laben's surprise set him several paces back, but he quickly recovered the composure to fire a shot into the big Indian shadow. Old Buck tottered, moaned, and fell dead.

Laben buried the body in a shallow grave and rode off on the prized auburn mare.

When spring came early, Laben plowed with the auburn mare and planted. Summer breathed fullness into the fields, butterflies spun through the fertile air. Autumn brought Laben the richest of harvests, the sweetest corn and heavy golden squash.

Then winter came, one late November dusk, with sneering winds and sleet like ice-locusts. At dinner that evening, Mary Blois, Laben's oldest daughter, said that she and a friend had been playing in the woods near where old Buck had lived, before his disappearance. She said, "He's back."

Laben's drumstick lodged in midair.

"We saw him in the woods, stark naked, dancing around with antlers strapped to his head."

"You're makin' that up!" Laben scolded.

"No, father, we saw him," Mary persisted.

Laben knew his daughter was not prone to untruths; still, he grew angry.

"You're mistaken, girl; that old Indian is gone."

The next morning Laben loaded his wagon with produce and his auburn mare towed him into the village. By afternoon the farmer's pockets were heavy with coins, more than they had ever known. Smiling, he set off for home.

It began to snow and his wagon creaked and rattled along through the wooded lanes. Steam came in bursts from the horse's nose and its big eyes blinked off heavy flakes of white.

Something in the woods made a deep crunching sound. Someone was moving in there! The auburn horse came to a stop. The wind moaned, "Laben . . ."

From out of the dense mist of snow there appeared a great stag, its antlers stabbing up at the belly of a gray winter night.

In the morning a man from the village, a Mr. J. Cushing, found Laben's wagon sitting in the center of the snowy road. Later on, at the village inn, he would report how he found Laben's body, broken and twisted in the snow, amidst telltale pink hoof prints.

He would also tell how he'd heard crashing in the woods and looked up to see Laben's auburn mare running off with a large male deer.

Pistols and Rain

Massachusetts, 1797

A Troubling Wound

Often the pain of another is little more than rumor, an intangible at best—a wound if the sufferer bears the good fortune of proof, yet even given that, our empathy for the sufferer's sensations remains an abstract. One cannot judge or measure his neighbor's suffering and so, agony, as it comes to us in words, is largely an object of faith. Who are we then to admonish William Howe for his medicinal indulgences?

Young and fond of ale, in the county of Essex by the sea, William found himself at one end of a dueling pistol with the end of another staring back at him. With surgeons hovering like crows in the field of lapping sea grass, the fine spring day hung clear above a sighing Atlantic.

The terror that arrives when one is suddenly called upon to scrutinize his own mortality was William's in quantity. He rattled in his boots as the breeze toyed with his cravat. His opponent, a veteran of honorable murder, stood straight and sure, holding his long pistol as if it were the handle of an umbrella.

Perhaps William's fear would have proved less keen had he possessed the presence of mind to ponder the odds he was facing. For all their smoke and noise, pistols of the day could not have proved more inaccurate were their shooters wrapped with blindfolds. Consequently, duels rarely ended with a mortality.

And so it went. William trembled, damp in sweat, his thoughts spinning so quickly that he could find no prayer in them. His gun barked and the smoke coughed out and his ball flew past his challenger like a shell returning to the sea.

The other's ball, while not even so large as a walnut, struck William with the force of a buffalo. He crumpled in the high windy grass, an ocean of pain filling his leg, overflowing up into his head—and everything in between. He groaned, looking at the blue sky, waiting for it to darken, which it never did. Voices moved closer and presently his surgeon towered above, a long, glum silhouette.

The surgeon took one look and turned to the others, announcing, "He breathes still."

Mercifully, William escaped the surgeon's saw, but it was months before he could stand and even longer before he was able to walk. Figuratively speaking, he ran—straight out of Essex and into the keeping of his uncle Ebenezer. His pain followed.

Every effort was made to relieve William's suffering, but neither the comforts that Ebenezer Howe's wealth supplied, nor the succession of doctors summoned to his bedside, could alleviate William's distress.

"There is nothing more to be done."

"I can do no more than I have."

"Terrible though it is to say...the injury persists fully against all manner of correction."

So concluded the healers.

William turned to drink. While others in the inns laughed, drumming unevenly upon the tables with their mugs, and stamping their boots on the worn wooden planks, William sat in stale corners brooding, ingesting numbing quantities until his driver came to carry him out.

Once, in Pierce's Tavern, William found himself in conversation with a strange traveler. While shabby and loud, the man sparked the interest of young Howe. It wasn't so much the fellow's manner as it was his boasting. Namely . . .

"Neither God in his clouds, nor Satan in his flames, has yet to devise an ill that I cannot remedy."

That had William by the ears.

The ensuing interchange informed William that this bedraggled stick of a man was well learned in the writings of the herbalist Culpeper, to say nothing of other, less orthodox methods of healing. Swift as a swallow, the man was whisked to Uncle Ebenezer's house.

The guest, Isaiah Dower, was genuinely impressed with his new friend's situation. Truth be told, the house—a lofty thing with massive twin chimneys—did indeed bear the note of wealth. The ornate woodwork, the paneled fireplace walls, the furnishings and rugs all provided an atmosphere of comfort and beauty afforded mainly to the prosperous. Dower was bathed and fed and offered a bed in the ell where the servants slept.

Light through the many panes cast squares of honey on the floor in William's chamber. He sat on the edge of his bed cringing down at his left leg.

"It's no use—the pain refuses to subside."

Dower, who only half sat on his chair, thinking that the dust of the road had imprinted upon his being and might somehow sully the cushion, leaned over the pitcher that held his latest concoction and sniffed.

"The quantity of chamomile is, perhaps, lacking," he speculated.

None of the herbal mixtures had proved effective in treating William's condition and he was pressed to doubt his visitor. It became increasingly evident that Dower's boasts were only so many idle words.

As the story goes, this latest amalgamation turned out to be the last, for that afternoon Uncle Ebenezer returned from town with word that the authorities were inquiring about Mr. Dower's whereabouts (for reasons that were never disclosed). In the morning the herbalist was not to be found, though he had slipped a piece of paper under William's door. It was a recipe of sorts.

The musty green of wormwood, married exactingly with fennel and anise. Distillation. *Absinthe.* Having afforded every effort to adhere to Dower's instructions, William came away with a green liquid, pale as peridot.

When at last this bitter brew was fit for consumption, and thus administered through the lips, William found himself hovering in the warmth of a verdant mist. He fumbled the glass onto a near table and slumped back upon his mattress. He smiled, for the pain was gone.

THE LAUGHTER OF AN ANGEL

Love, like pain, arrives in any season . . . when spring is a garden of perfume and bees, or when the moon is a snowball and November handles the woods with spare, russet gloves. It was at this later time, following the blare and blaze of October, that New England became a somber thing. The stark, near-stripped woods stood so dense that they made a gray mist of the hills. The sky, kindred in shade, might have been a misplaced Atlantic, the color of a slate over which a carver would hunch, chipping out: IN MEMORY OF.

In this time of pheasants and unobstructed wind, Uncle Ebenezer's house bore the contrasting flush of music and laughter common to balls. Two adjoining chambers on the north side of the second floor became one as dividing panels were swung up against the ceiling and furnishings were cleared to make room for dance.

Below and by himself in the west parlor, William scowled at the beating of feet above his head. The sound taunted him as he slumped in a window seat, cool panes pressed to his back. His dark hat was squashed under his arm like a dead crow.

A guest poked his wig in and, tamping a pipe, inquired, "Will you not join in the dance, young Mr. Howe?"

William pointed to his leg and grinned dryly.

"Ahhh—sorry!" The man's head withdrew and he trotted up the stairs.

Sustained by his medicine, William was just capable of socializing, but the leg was little more than a weight to drag—a hollow vessel full of green liquid. The young man was mobile enough, certainly, but dancing was now relegated to memory and dream.

More footsteps sounded in the hall, a skirt hissing like wind-blown leaves over the wide boards. The steps were softer than the previous intruder's. William knew that they belonged to a woman even before he saw one drift past. He sat up on his seat and returned the passing gaze of Elizabeth Fay.

Softer than candlelight, the young woman might have been a ghost, William thought, the way she floated past and on up the stairs as if there were only a spring breeze beneath her gown. And her face—ideal beyond the limitations of corporeality—was quiet as the pale moon. Her hair was teased to a framing nimbus as if dawn were rising behind her head. And while her mouth was a small unopened rose and her nose was fine, it was Elizabeth's eyes that imprinted themselves in William's mind. They were like a Grecian sea deep enough to sink ships, or twin drops of diaphanous peridot. He wanted to drink them.

Green mist swirled in the man's head when he stood. He grabbed his cane and limped after the ghost, precariously managing the stairs. The music grew louder and his heart, too, like the many stomping feet. Once in the upper hallway, he leaned in the doorway of the ballroom and spotted Elizabeth going gracefully about her steps.

Young men were about her like flies and each more stylish than William, more handsome, or so he thought. They were all skilled in their movements, the products of dance masters, no doubt. Their frocks were of the perfect materials and their lower legs, from knee to ankle, were white in silk stockings, like spry candles. Unable to join them, William hovered dizzily in the doorframe, his heart staring out from a prison of ribs.

He loved her immediately. He loved her green eyes, her retiring smile, and her laughter (above the strings and stomps) was that of an angel. He loved her from her head—like a crown of dandelion spores honeyed with light—down to her feet, like timid sparrows peeking out from a rim of lace as intricate as hoarfrost.

A BITTER KISS

The day mustered its light and crept upward, westward behind a thatch of skinny maples. William took his medicine, then his tea, and then a stroll in the brisk, bleak November afternoon.

Most of the leaves were down, though here and there the rusty oaks showed stubbornly among brittle brown counterparts. Small birds, high in their green pine chapels, prayed noisily for a safe trip south.

It was by no mistake that William found himself outside the home of Elizabeth Fay. Elizabeth's father—The Captain—had done well for himself and the house stood as evidence. It was tall and white and rectangular, with two great chimneys. The front and side doors boasted classically inspired flattened pillars and projecting pediments that were drawn-out triangles. A line of molding like large wooden teeth ran beneath the eaves.

Soft green light played in William's head as he hesitated by the fence. A mumble of pain came from his left leg, a consequence of the hike. He reached into his great coat and found a flask. The bitter relief was barely past his lips when the door of the house opened and a servant girl appeared. She spoke, "Excuse me, sir . . . Miss Elizabeth wonders if, upon such a chill day, you might like to come in for a cup of hot tea."

William stuffed his medicament away and straightened.

"Tea? Yes, why certainly! Yes, yes, tea would be delightful."

William limped into the house behind the girl and there stood Elizabeth with her serene stare. He plucked off his tricorn and bowed.

"Good day, young miss," William said.

"Good day," Elizabeth returned, curtsying, "I just now saw you from the window. You would be the nephew of Mister Ebenezer Howe, unless I am incorrect?"

"That I am. I be William Howe, formerly of Salem, in Essex."

"Ahh. Would you care to join me in tea?"

For a moment the man could only stare, his breathing constricted by the proximity of beauty. Her words came to him, but they were more heat than sound.

"Tea, William . . . would you care for tea?"

"Tea—yes. Of course, that would be splendid."

He followed Elizabeth past the doorway of a parlor where he saw a cleaning girl sweeping severed fingers from the brick hearth and a crow composed of flame flit up behind the logs in the firebox. Elizabeth seemed not to notice and William rubbed at his eyes.

There had never been a kinder hostess. Elizabeth proved as charming as she was bashful. Gifted in wit and manners, she fascinated William. She blushed readily and her laughter, as noted, was an angel's.

They sat quietly for a time, only peeking at each other, then, with a boldness that might have come from his flask, William leaned forward, holding Elizabeth's eye and whispered, "It is my dearest hope, one day, to have the very good fortune to kiss you."

Elizabeth pinkened and hid her smile with a hand, though her peridot stare was meaningful. "I think I should like that."

The kiss came soon enough. It was slow, an ember's warmth, a vestige of October to temper the November cold. On a brown road, by a gray wood, with the blue sky above, they embraced. The young man's lips tasted of wormwood, like a forest's bitter shadows, yet something awakened in Elizabeth's heart.

A Speck of Rust

Over time, the pain determined to increase, and William found himself downing more of his elixir to subdue it. The first snow had scattered, but the cold it represented and the roughness of the road neither deterred nor greatly discomforted William, for his flask was at the ready. On this particular morning he set out jauntily, despite the numb weight of his left leg.

His thoughts were all about Elizabeth's flesh, which he had come to know in intimate terms. It had happened as simply and naturally as rain might, when the day least expected it. The afternoon had been cool and gray and their lips had been too busy finding the other's to shape words. The barn afforded convenient shelter and the hay offered a bed.

Her youthfulness had been disclosed in full, its pallor and warmth, its softness and contours. Her breasts were as firm as pears and her nipples hard like candle nubs. He had kissed all, from the swan-white neck down to warm hair the blond of August rye. He even pressed his mouth to a small mole—a coy speck of rust—on the back of her left shoulder.

LIKE BEASTS, OR DEMONS

It was not so much that William was ignorant of the particulars so far as fashion went, it was that he resented the restrictions affixed to conformity. Even so, love has a peculiar way of altering the will, and this morning William would present himself anew, dressed as well as any of those charming young fellows at the ball. He went so far as to wonder if the right quantity of his medicine might, over time, see him dancing as they had that night he first saw Elizabeth.

These thoughts and others came about in a hopeful way, for Elizabeth had sparked a light within him where none had shone before.

On his way to Captain Fay's house, he paused to inspect his reflection in a puddle. While the water was a muddy gray, he stared back at himself, handsome enough in his suit of imported black velvet, with his white satin vest and cocked hat. His silver knee and shoe buckles gleamed as if shaped from stars.

William went directly to the Fay property. The morning air was scented with hay and fresh-cut wood as he came alongside the out-buildings. He was humming happily, but there were sounds coming from within the barn that caused him to stop and listen.

Were his ears now playing tricks? Wasn't it enough that he was spying burning birds in fireplaces and body parts where none should be? That very morning he had glimpsed a toe poking out from his tea like an albino toad.

He moved closer and pressed an ear to the door. No, it was more than his imagination—he could hear grunting and groaning from inside, as if the barn were filled with beasts and demons.

William eased the door open a crack and stared in. The first thing he saw, there in the dimness, was Captain Fay's fine great coat flung across the rail of a horse stall. Looking harder, he saw pale figures, down in the matted hay. A bare woman was astride a man who lay grunting beneath. The woman went up and down, and while her hair was hidden by a bonnet, he saw a small reddish mark there on the back of her left shoulder.

William gasped and lurched away, hurrying back onto the road, his head and heart aswirl in a mutual fever—the door swung shut behind him and made a noise.

The Captain cursed and pulled the woman down out of view, dislodging her bonnet in the process so that her dark hair spilled onto his chest. The fleck of red oak leaf that had been stuck to the maid's shoulder fell loose and disappeared into the hay.

THE CHALLENGE

About the time that The Captain and Mrs. Fay and their five daughters were taking their evening meal, an uninvited visitor marched into their house and burst through the door of the chamber where they sat. All eyes went to young William. Even Elizabeth was alarmed by his manner.

Thrusting a finger at the head of the house, William spat, "You, sir, are a pig."

A communal huff flew from the women. The Captain shot up, indignant, bear-like.

William was not quite finished. "You lie with your own daughter as if with a common harlot!"

The missus gave a cry and her hand flew to her chest like a small white bird.

"Out!" The Captain roared. "Out with you!"

William turned to glare at Elizabeth. "And you," he hissed, "your vulgarity shames all women. You, miss, have made a black thing of my heart."

With that William wheeled and limped from the room, nearly tripping over severed arms as Elizabeth collapsed against her mother, sobbing.

In the gray light of a November morning, when the fields were shrouded in frost, a knocking fell upon Ebenezer Howe's door. A gentleman was admitted and taken to see William. This visitor, Thomas Sumner, was operating as "second" on behalf of Captain Fay, with whom he shared an equality of social rank. Sumner let William know that the Captain demanded satisfaction, and if no apology were forthcoming then the insulted party would require William's presence for a duel.

Though groggy and still slumped in his nightshirt, William summoned defiance. "If you would, please inform The Captain that nothing like an apology will pass from these lips."

The rigid Mr. Sumner regarded William impassively. "Then it falls upon me to offer you the choice of weapon."

"Pistols," William said. "I choose pistols."

A Death in the Field

The challenged had chosen the place, a field as bleak as all November, situated within a far horseshoe of low russet brush, with dim woods beyond that. The woods consisted mainly of stark and moss-worn maples and young birches like abandoned crutches.

A low mist floated above the damp discolored grass as if smoke after a battle. Fey crows spoke off in the wood, their voices hollow, tinged with anticipation; some sprang up off the field like great black flowers when two coaches arrived on the scene.

Solemn figures stepped down from the carriages, the separate parties conferring at opposite ends of the expanse. At length the seconds walked to meet each other at the center and it was confirmed that William remained fixed against apology.

With no friends to speak of in that part of the world, William relied on his dear Uncle Ebenezer to act as his second. Ebenezer saw to it that a surgeon was on hand. Captain Fay's party consisted of Thomas Sumner and a surgeon named Beals, who was a bespectacled cauldron with a wig the color of frost.

The Captain was a serious sight, tall and steady in his great coat, his eyes set in a determined squint, though the sun was barely above the trees and clouds hung in the sky like the wings of drowned angels. He was a veteran of honorable murder.

The seconds readied the pistols while the duelists counted their paces. Uncle Ebenezer watched woefully as his nephew limped along. Beals checked his watch impatiently and took a pinch of snuff. When the pistols were charged, the seconds gave one another a stiff nod and walked off for their men.

It was only the second time that William had worn his nice new clothing; despite these garments, and the knee-length woolen great coat he wore over them, he found himself shivering. The Captain saw this and smirked.

Uncle Ebenezer had reached his kin and he offered the open pistol case, whispering, "Good luck be with you, my boy."

William could only nod. He seemed dazed as he selected one of the long heavy flintlocks. It was an unpretentious thing with an octagonal barrel, iron mounts, and a walnut stock.

Captain Fay plucked up his weapon, which was elegantly fitted with a brass barrel and engraved silver mounts. It glinted as the sun tried to squeeze through the clouds.

William mistook the drumming of hooves for the sound of his heart. A small black buggy appeared through the mist and rattled onto the field. When it came to a stop the horse snorted and Elizabeth climbed out.

The Captain was flustered by her arrival; he turned and barked as she floated to where Sumner and Beals stood. "Good heavens, go home, Elizabeth!"

"I will not." She stood defiant. The young woman was no less stubborn than her father, as he knew too well.

"Well," he softened, "cover your eyes then. Shant be pretty, this."

Elizabeth gazed at one man then the other. Her heart was for them both. While she did not cover her eyes, her hands were cupped over her mouth as if anticipating a scream.

And so it went. The pistols were cocked, the sound crisp in the open air, like a twig under a boot. The men stood sideways, just six yards apart, as they raised their weapons and pointed at each other.

Dizziness flooded William and he turned his head ever so slightly to look once more upon Elizabeth's beauty. He felt a tear on his face, but could not see her tears for the distance between them. She stood off to the side with Thomas Sumner and the round surgeon.

It fell upon Ebenezer to give the order. "Fire!" he called.

In that instant William found his target. His pistol thundered and the cloud from the weapon obscured that of his opponent's. The Captain's shot struck him square in the knee, inches below the old wound.

William's aim proved more exact—the ball tore straight through Elizabeth's chest and flew off with the crows that spat startled from the brush.

"I'm killed!" the woman gasped, crumpling to the ground.

William himself lay in the cool wet grass, clutching his bloody leg. The pain was a molten ocean. His surgeon and Uncle Ebenezer lifted him and stumbled over to their carriage. They struggled to get him into the thing and then sped off for the parsonage down the road. Once there, the surgeon, left with no other alternative, amputated William's left leg. Thank heavens the young duelist had kept his medicine on hand.

Elizabeth died in the field.

November Rain

Once, in the cheerless gray of November, when the year was limping toward snow, it rained. It rained on the town (far from the Bay Colony) where William had fled to evade the law. It was a green rain and it drummed on his roof and wept at his windows, and in the morning, following the storm, the puddles were like mud and peridot and each bore a face. A woman's face.

The Recurrent Silence

Dear Michael,

Please give this a read, and when you have some time, let me know what you think. It's a piece my dear Aunt Lydia was working on when she died last spring. Knowing that I shared her interest in genealogy and a love of New England history, she left me a number of books and papers on the subjects, this among them. On the surface, it appears to be the history of a small town here in the north-central part of the state, but there is something curious about it. I won't say just what this strange thing is, however, until the end . . .

A HISTORY OF NORTHMINSTER
By Lydia Purcell

An hour's ride up from Worcester, traveling westward along the Old Athol Road, you will encounter the quaint Massachusetts town of Northminster. It is an easy target to miss, however, even for those seeking it, for it is secreted in a dense pine wood that straddles the New Hampshire border. Still largely a farming community, it retains much of its past charm and offers some fine examples of Colonial architecture.

Laid out as a township in 1734, Northminster had few inhabitants originally. Some notable characters from those early days would include Cyrus Goodwin (the carpenter who went on to erect the First Parish Church), the Rev. Elias Brooks, and the farmer Tobias Martin, whose frame house still stands on a knoll by Otter Pond.

Rev. Brooks's father James came over from Bury Saint Edmonds, County Suffolk, England in 1643 (he was still in his infancy at the time). This elder Brooks served a tour of duty as a captain in King Phillip's War (1675–76). He married Dorotha Rugg of Sudbury and together they had ten children. Church records show that he died of bilious fever at Fitchburg in 1710.

In 1735, one hundred veterans of King Phillip's War (or their heirs) were awarded 40-acre house lots in Northminster, in honor of their loyal service to the crown. Rev. Elias Brooks was granted his father's share and built there the first parsonage. This building was lost to fire in 1773; the second was built in 1775 and stands to this day. It is a handsome work of Georgian symmetry, with massive twin chimneys and heavy pediments above the front and side entrances.

Elias married Asa Trowbridge, a tanner's daughter, the year that the first parsonage went up. Silence, the first of their seven children, was born in November 1736. The other children were as follows:

> Thankful, born 1737
> Jonah, born 1739
> Solomon, born 1741
> Gideon, born 1742
> Jedediah, born 1744
> Prudence, born 1746

A series of terrible misfortunes diminished the ranks of Rev. Brooks' family, starting with young Silence (of whom a portrait, in remarkable condition, remains in the keeping of the Northminster Historical Society). At the age of five, she fell into a tanning pit and drowned. Her headstone can be found at the Old Burying Ground on the Northminster Common.

In February of 1740, three-year-old Thankful fell ill with winter fever. Suffering delirium, she reported seeing her sister Silence sitting on the edge of her bed. Neighbors tried healing Thankful with medicinal herbs to no effect, so the physician was summoned, he being William Upham (who was also Justice of the Peace). Dr. Upham immediately drew his lancet from a small black pocket case and bled the patient. When his best efforts failed to bring about any positive change, the most religious men in town were gathered to pray for the child. None of these measures managed to save her, though, for she perished that night.

More adversity came in the spring of 1745, when young Jonah was badly injured under the wheels of a cart. He lived for several days after the accident, and in his fever reported seeing Silence sitting at the end of his bed. He was just five years of age.

Solomon and Gideon both were lost that December, struck with consumption. Neither lived to see his fourth year.

Two years later, Jedediah drowned in the sawmill's pond at the age of three.

Only Prudence survived to adulthood. While she never married, she had some small degree of fame afforded her by the locals for being the first in town to be in possession of a spinet. She exhibited remarkable musical ability, and in her later years played organ at the First Parish Church.

Prudence delighted many with her playing and good-natured personality. This is noted in her diary, where she notes that relations and neighbors from surrounding towns came to hear her as she sat at her instrument in the parlor. One can read about her musical enthusiasm in her diary, which is preserved at the Historical Society (which contains a great number of old journals, reports, and various documents made available to the public for viewing).

Townsfolk from as far away as Lancaster mourned when Prudence died. Some wept when they saw the silent spinet sitting in the Brooks parlor. She had just turned thirty years old when the dreadful illness came upon her. Her flesh wilted; the disease wore down her body, and yet her spirit remained bright to the end. When her suffering was over, Prudence was laid to rest a mile east of the parsonage, at the Old Burying Ground. There she would rest among kin. Rev. Ebenezer Young of Phillipston attended the burial.

"Silence fell over the whole town that bitter April morn," Rev. Young noted in his papers. "So quiet was the day that the birds were without song as they sat in the trees like sad dark fruit.

They knew, perhaps, that one terribly fond of their music was gone." The Brooks house was opened to friends and relatives after the burial. Prudence, with her playing and joviality, and in her kindhearted ways had touched all of their lives. Even as the mourners walked away from the grave (there alongside those of her siblings, all gone before her), they traded fond memories.

The Poor Rev. Brooks, returning to his home, wept quietly to himself. His sad arthritic body was too weak even to stand, so he sat wordlessly at the spinet. His tears fell on the pale keys.

Was it perhaps the loss of Rev. Brooks' daughter Prudence, his last child who had only been gone a matter of months, that hastened the fellow's own demise? He took ill not long after she died. But for his beloved Asa, the man had felt terribly alone, though his faith in God remained strong. There in the parsonage he retired to his bedchamber, suffering from a burning fever. His thoughts were plagued by the memories of earlier losses.

The man was bedridden for a week. Delirious, he laughed and wept and even drew several skulls on his bedcovers. One night he told Asa that Silence had come to sit on the edge of the bed. Of course that was only the madness of disease; the illness had taken his mind. He lived another five days before succumbing on the first day of August in 1776.

Small gray headstones, carved from flaky New England slate, mark the graves where the children of Rev. Elias Brooks and his wife Asa are buried at Northminster's Old Burying Ground. In the earth along with them lay their parents, the family reunited. Asa died in the winter of 1779. Her final days were spent alone at her beloved parsonage. She was eulogized by the Rev. John Coffin as a fine mother and a faithful wife.

That is as far as my Aunt Lydia got in compiling her history of Northminster. It's an accurate piece, so far as I can tell, but I mentioned to you that there was something peculiar about it. This strange aspect was pointed out by a friend of mine (don't ask me how he ever noticed!). Go back to the above history and count seven paragraphs up from the bottom. You'll come to the sentence that reads *Prudence delighted many with her playing and with her good-natured personality.* Starting with the word *Prudence* read down the rest of the history, sticking only to the left most word of each line. Oddly enough, you will find what (coincidentally?) seems to be an addendum of sorts.

Best regards,
Benjamin Read

The Collector in the Mill

There was nothing of particular interest about the room itself; while it was not spacious, it was clean and the rent reasonable. The house rules prohibiting guests were not unacceptable, for I, a bachelor in the midst of pursuing a degree in archaeology, was not inclined to entertain visitors.

The room offered a place to sleep and study, thus my needs were sated. The only interesting aspect to the room was the view.

The towering old tenement in which I was a boarder stood on the edge of a once vigorous industrial block on the city's east side. Abandoned mills crowded the narrow streets where puddles hid in potholes and reticent natives passed hurriedly without interchange. One of these brick monstrosities stood directly parallel to my room. Architecturally speaking, it was not unlike so many other oversized, angular structures of the time when mills lined up along the oily river that cut through the eastern quarter of the city. It had long, dark windows and precarious fire escapes fastened to its side, these being so encrusted with rust that they were, in color, virtually the same as the bricks. Some of the windows had been boarded up following an explosion and fire some years back.

I had been staying in the rooming house on Danvers Street for several days before I took note of anything abnormal about the abandoned mill. After hours of pressing my spectacles into a ponderous tome on prehistory, I rose and paced my chamber, stretching my limbs and rubbing at my eyes. I happened, upon chance, to glance out through the window at the mill across the way.

It had been raining steadily for several hours and the building appeared darker than usual as it stood in the evening gloom. I was about to return to my studies when a lightning flash illuminated the mill and I saw, through one of the long smeary windows, something large and circular, perhaps the span of a wagon wheel, blink past the glass.

While intrigued, I decided that there were a number of factors with which to explain away the occurrence as a natural phenomenon. Perhaps the glare of light had illuminated a silvery trashcan lid, propped in the empty building, or possibly some forsaken piece of machinery that had suffered damage in the explosion and ensuing flames that had led to the building's uninhabited state.

At any rate, I was not alarmed, and gave the matter little thought in the immediate days that followed.

The city's eastern side was a place of squalor, overall; the unfortunate seemed to gravitate there as if magnetized to the chill shadows and damp streets and crumbling doorways of ancient houses. On my way home from the university, I encountered many sad, bedraggled types. They were furtive creatures by and large, pitiful and unkempt. Most seemed ill, and, curiously enough, a notable number of them appeared short one or another limb. I made a habit of carrying coins to clink into their hungry cups.

It was just after dusk, one cool Monday in autumn, when I made my way down Danvers, having taken several shortcuts through the maze of alleys in the mill district. An unsettling howling sound came from a clump of shrubbery set back on the lawn of a moldering Colonial several doors down from my residence.

I paused to see what the source of the painful emission might be, then walked closer, crouching to peer into the shadowy vegetation. It gave me quite a scare when a scraggly cat came bounding out, wild-eyed and hissing, dashing past me, heading down the street. The poor beast moved with a great deal of speed considering it was missing a leg.

It rained quite frequently that autumn I spent on Danvers Street, but the weather was not a cause of great distress, so far as I was concerned. While I tried to occupy myself with my scholastic goals, I became increasingly unsettled, despite the fact that there seemed to be no actual source of disturbance. It is true that I was gazing more frequently at the brooding mill across the street, but I could perceive no connection between the place and my disquieted state.

There was, I suppose, a curious foreboding quality about the mill, and I had noted the way pigeons (more than common atop other old buildings in the area) avoided lighting on the place. But I could identify no logical reason to be spending so much time peering out at it.

My schoolwork suffered further interruption when one of my classmates from the university inexplicably vanished. Morris Webster was, for the most part, a satisfactory student, though his overt interest in women seemed a near constant source of folly both inside and outside the campus grounds.

I had last spoken to Webster the afternoon before he came up missing. Following our final class of the afternoon, we had ducked into a small diner to escape a chill downpour, and to warm our innards with coffee. My companion was in a state of intense enthusiasm, having made a particular appointment with a comely young waitress he had met at a local eatery.

Webster had recently been threatened with eviction from the house where he was boarding after violating a "no visitors" condition. He had lamented for days and spent a great deal of time discussing alternative locations where an amorous young male might find privacy with an attractive young waitress.

My friend was in high spirits that rainy afternoon, having come to what he considered a satisfactory conclusion, so far as his dilemma was concerned. I was skeptical about his choice, and told him as much, but Webster was as stubborn as he was amorous, and he would not be persuaded by one endowed with as little argumentative endurance as I possessed.

So, when we parted, each heading off into the rain-heavy dusk, he was his usual lighthearted self, grinning with boyish charm. I, for the life of me, could not imagine why a young woman would care to join Webster, or anyone else for that matter, in an old deserted factory, but then he had insisted that the young lady was enthusiastic about the idea of stealing into one of the local decrepit mills, providing it offered them a level of privacy.

Neither Webster's landlord, nor his friends, myself included, were terribly concerned when he did not report to his room that night, or to class the following morning. He was, after all, known to indulge his restless nature. It was the young woman's family who contacted the police.

Searches were made in some of the abandoned mills (though I saw no one enter the one facing my room) on the assumption that the couple had become trapped, or fallen through weakened floorboards in one of the brick behemoths. The authorities were hopeful and attempted to persuade the families of the missing couple that it was only a matter of time before they were discovered.

Three days passed before a boy delivering newspapers made a tragic and gruesome discovery. He found the body of the girl lying on the gray bank of the rancid river that crawled along through the unwholesome shadows of the mill district. She was face down in the mud where she had either crawled, or been murdered. Her left arm had been severed at the elbow.

The police worked tirelessly in their attempt to locate Webster, on the suspicion that he was responsible for the terrible violence perpetrated against the girl. It was theorized that he had killed her and then departed from the city, which would explain why none had seen him since he and the girl went about their nocturnal adventure.

If Webster was not responsible for the crime, then his disappearance might indicate that he, too, had fallen prey to murderous force. Wasn't it possible that the killer or killers had intended to discard the bodies in the dark waters of the river, and had been interrupted before completing the task, thus leaving the girl on the bank?

A search was made, but the murky current offered no answers. Webster's body was not found, nor was a murder weapon, for that matter. Several large leg bones were discovered, but they were certainly not human, and they seemed very old indeed.

No arrest was made in the case of the murdered waitress, and Morris Webster, so far as investigators were concerned, remained a suspect. But no one knew where he was, or if he was even alive.

Several months passed and even the coming of snow could not brighten the dreary streets of the mill district. Each day I passed the homeless and destitute, huddled on door stoops, or hobbling in the gray slush of the gutters. The miserable beasts wandered hungrily in the crippling cold.

While I had resumed my studies, I was further fascinated with the building upon which my window gazed, and went so far as to question my landlord about its history.

The old man, while never striking me as loquacious, gave the impression that he was reluctant to speak on the subject—until I provided him with a bottle of whiskey and saw to it that he consumed a good portion.

It was only then that he told me about the retired professor who had purchased the vacant mill in the months preceding the explosion. The man's name was Reynolds and he had just returned to the states from an excursion in the Middle East. He was a solitary fellow, rarely seen except for those nights when his spindly silhouette passed back and forth before the upper-floor windows of the mill where he worked and slept.

No one knew what went on behind the brick walls of the old mill, but it was assumed that the man was involved in some form of laboratory research. Reynolds did not make himself available to questions; he shunned human contact.

I asked the landlord about the explosion and he steeled himself with another drink. He gazed into the amber bottle and muttered something about screams. I urged him to elaborate and he told me that he had been awakened by screaming, coming from the mill, moments before an explosion shook the place and sent fire raging through the second floor. Reynolds died in the blast. Some of his limbs were never found. The building had stood empty since.

Some months later it became known that authorities from the Middle East had been attempting to locate the mysterious professor in order to question him about the disappearance of some pages from an ancient book in a museum where he had been conducting research.

The passages from the manuscript known as *The Scorched Book* contained archaic rites alleged to give one the power to "crack space," I thought it ironic that the stolen pages of *The Scorched Book* were lost in a storm of flame.

For a number of weeks I spent my free time wading through musty corridors of books, haunting this or that library, searching for information on the mill, Professor Reynolds, and *The Scorched Book*. Considering the amount of time invested, the information I collected hardly quenched my curiosity.

The mill had no prior history of infamy; in fact, nothing out of the ordinary had occurred there until Reynolds purchased it. I located some papers that the professor had written on ancient systems of magic, but they were teasingly brief, ambiguous things concerning mystical symbols and strange herbal potations. As for *The Scorched Book*, I came across a solitary reference to it in a creaking old tome of esoteric matters. *The Scorched Book*, it was noted, was written in a code, most of which remained untranslated. Anyone opening its pages was encouraged to leave a drop of their blood on the final page as something of a toll price to ensure safe departure from the thing. Whoever refused, or neglected to offer the placating libation, risked grave misfortune. So said the reference book.

Winter had settled in about the lonely streets of the mill district, tucking snow into the windy alleys, leaving half-melted clumps on the crooked roofs of tilted houses. The puddles in the pot holes dotting the narrow stretch of Danvers Street had glazed darkly and even the sluggish waters of that fetid black river had filmed with sickly gray ice.

I discovered the skeletal remains of a dog half-sunk in a heap of snow along the outer side wall of the mill that loomed across from my temporary home. It was a nightmarish thing to behold, the bare teeth and eye sockets blurred with ice and the front legs poking out as if it had made an effort of digging itself free.

I stared at the ghastly thing for several minutes and then a whispering impulse came to my mind and I indulged it, digging at the snow with my hands until the whole of the remains were revealed. It was as I had suspected—the dog was missing a hind leg.

Digging further in the snow, I at last uncovered a cellar window where the boards had been loosened, probably by disenfranchised street urchins seeking shelter in the old mill, as it seems the unfortunate hound had done.

I peered into the low rectangular darkness of the window and a dreadful chill flew through my bones. The window exhaled a foul odor, like the ghost of something burnt, and I made away quickly, gulping at the cold air, hugging my coat about my flesh. I did not stop running until I was locked safely in the familiar warmth of my room.

Following my discovery of an ingress into the mill, and in light of the unnerving sense of dread that fired through me at the time, I made a concerted effort to avoid looking out at the sullen mass of bricks across from my room on Danvers Street. I kept my shades drawn against the thing and turned my head from it when on the street, all the while striving against the swelling urge to go to the place and access the secrets that waited in the dark beyond its walls.

There was little doubt in my mind that there was something more than silence and webs in the abandoned building. Still, I possessed no tangible evidence on which to base such speculation; it was intuition more than reason that formulated my opinion.

I held fast against the compulsion to explore the mill, though I could not entirely eliminate its presence from my mind. I found myself doodling the dark brick-lipped cellar window on my papers in class and on the newspapers sprawled across the desk in my quarters, where I had aimed to anchor my thoughts in occurrences beyond the grim streets and hollow factories that surrounded my little room.

The sky was a sickly thing above the city as I traded the warmth and comfort of the university for the gray of twilight. I walked briskly, bundled against the wind that raged with teeth of sleet. The haggard Colonial houses seemed to huddle together against the climate, squeezing the streets that took me to the grime and dimness of the mill district.

I chose an uncommon route in order to lessen the length of time in which the icy precipitation could sink its chill into my limbs. I stumbled through treacherous alleys, over heaps of darkness that might have been debris, or miserable humans with no means with which to rent a roof, sheltering under soggy blankets.

It was in just such a place, where the freezing rain had transformed the dark walls into glistening reptilian things, that a ragged figure lurched up from the cluttered floor and turned to me with a face of horror. Though hunger had sunken the features in shadow, and the hair had gone wild, and whiskers crowded the gaping mouth, I recognized the face of Morris Webster. The charm and wit that had once gleamed in the man's eyes were gone. There was only desperation, or a feral madness that I found both pitiful and frightening. I spoke his name, but he recoiled, turned and ran, muttering incoherently, flailing his left arm, the right sleeve flapping as if there was nothing inside of it.

I tried to pursue, but I slipped repeatedly on the slick pavement and Morris's twisted silhouette vanished into the shadows and sleet of the labyrinthine alleys.

Squinting against the weather, I reeled through a maze of narrow passages that bent the wind into odd sounds. The cold air ached in my lungs and, when at last I paused to catch my breath, I realized that I was lost. I cursed and thrust myself onward, turning down this and that alley, my feet squishing in unidentified substances that reeked of stagnancy and rot. I felt as if I was trapped in the petrified innards of some immense monstrosity.

My feet flew from under me, betrayed again by the icy pavement, and I found myself flat on my chest, my face close to something familiar. It was the dark cellar window of the Danvers Street mill, with the rotting boards that once had served to seal it dangling ineffectually.

The vile breath of the mill burned in my nostrils and my previous concerns wisped away. It mattered not that I had been lost, that Morris Webster had escaped into the night; nothing mattered, beyond squeezing my body past the boards into the brick opening that led into the bowels of the mill.

It would be a misrepresentation of the truth were I to maintain that, finding myself within the very object of my fascination, I did not experience a strange sort of thrill. It was a blend of fear and curiosity such as I had never known. I stood in the dizzying darkness of that vast, dank under-chamber while my limbs prickled with gooseflesh.

The floor beneath the window was littered with coins and shoes, lending the impression that they had been lost by individuals either hastily or carelessly leaving the premises. I found a box of matches there and struck one to take in my surroundings.

What a dismal place it was! There were web-laced pipes in rusty disarray spanning the low ceiling, and a huddled mass of tanks and tubes that had once been a boiler. Brick-colored smears ran across the dusty floor from the bottom of a staircase to the window through which I had come.

My match burnt out and I found myself in creaking darkness, feet carrying me toward the stairs that would take me up to ground level. The old boards ached loudly beneath my weight as I ascended, trembling so that the match sticks rattled in their box.

I made my way through a series of abandoned offices, each like a tomb and infested with that heady stench, as if the air itself was scorched. Dull light made a ghostly effort to penetrate the tall window panes, but it only served to dilute the darkness and I found myself thankful there were no furnishings to stumble over.

In that gloomy series of compartments I became aware of a certain vibration beneath my feet, as if the sprawling structure were trembling upon the rising tide of an earthquake, or situated near to a stretch of railroad tracks, which was not the case. Next there came a sound from the floor above me that set my heart reeling in my chest and sent my blood swirling feverishly through my skull. The heavy, grinding roar lasted only seconds, yet it was so loud and close that it seemed as if several train cars had rolled through the second story of the mill.

Had I not been so morbidly enthralled, I'd have heeded the rational voice in my head, which urged me to leave, but I was not powered by logic at the time and made my way up the steep, black-smeared stairs that slanted toward the second floor.

My match flared in the blackness of that great brick enclosure; it was a feeble light at best, and it only hinted at the ash-stained walls and twisted upright shapes that stood at uneven intervals in the room. At last I was within the space where I had glimpsed that mysterious circular object through the long window, several months previous. My match burnt down; I lit another and proceeded.

The air pressed upon me with its smoky stench as sleet clicked and rasped at the windows, and the tall geometrically irregular shapes came into sharper focus.

They were boxes, I discovered; tall, crazily constructed boxes comprised of greenish planks of some unknown wood. I could find no screws or nails holding the things together, yet they resisted my attempts to loosen them to see what they contained.

I lit another match and peered between several of the boards into one of the crates, and discovered a haphazard heap of pale bones. They were packed into the crude box, which towered several feet above me and stretched wider than my arms. There were human bones and cat bones and dog bones and bones from creatures that I had no awareness of, all knotted in a frenzied nest.

While gazing down at a set of finger bones, curling out from a gap in the boards, it struck me that each of these remains came from a hand, or foot, or arm, or leg, or paw, as the case may be.

Without hesitation I turned and ran, pounding on the old wooden floor, fear raging through me as I aimed for the steep stairs that led down to the floor below.

Once more I felt the building quake and heard that dreadful noise, and there before me in the dark of that unholy mill appeared a great smoky mass, twitching with snake-like protrusions, staring with one gigantic eye in which many pupils darted like fish in a tank.

The roar of a train drowned out my screams.

My fascination with the mill has been sated at last. I am no longer compelled to gaze at it, nor do I feel the urge to go inside of it. I have communed with it, as others before me have, and I am changed by the convergence. I have not paid my rent in weeks, nor have I attended a single class; I have sat half-starved, nourished only by scraps of sleep, in my room on Danvers Street, training myself to write with my left hand.

As these scrawled words prove, I have progressed with some degree of success, and now my story is complete. But, I fear there are only hours remaining before what is left of my sanity falters and I find myself haunting the alleyways and shadows of the dank and soulless mill district, like the others who have lost their limbs and their minds to that collector in the mill.

Marcy Waters

Massachusetts, 1859

Marcy Waters. How I remember her now, standing by the bank of the river, with the summer light warm on the current of east-bound water and in the swift current of blood beneath her white skin. She lifted her skirt to show me where the briars had bit at her ankles and she laughed, tossing her long red hair, squinting her summer-green eyes.

We were both just ten, both stumbling between the inner world of dreams and the outer world, with its many colors and its slow days and the confusing ache of impatience. If there were, indeed, a world beyond our small New England town, it was only in pictures and other people's words. We knew the shapes of the seasons well enough, though . . . the cold-quilted hours of snow, the rusted glory of apple-fat autumn, spring like a garden of colored ghosts, and summers that seemed unending, the hot days stitched together by lightning.

Somewhere on a hill, east of a great swamp full of swallowing shadows, we sat and told stories of Indian spirits that moved like deer.

Marcy swore she saw one once when rain flew down from Canada and geese in great numbers fidgeted on old John Whitney's fields. Crouched as a spider and swift as a fox, it flitted in and out of wet shadows.

Another time, she had me believe, they were in the trees about her house, with the owls. I told her she was a liar and she cried and when next we spoke, she showed me a box made of strange gray wood. There were patterns in the grain of wood, like owls or skulls or soft watery things that only walk this earth in dreams.

She found it in May, when John Whitney died in that queer accident. It was behind the woodpile where he'd been chopping. She hid it all summer, while blackberries peered out from their thorny vines and climbed crazily over cool stone walls. It was only when September brought soft rain and squirrels that she dug it out from the hollow log where it had sheltered. Only then did she hear the birds inside, and feel their eager flutters, unborn against the wood.

Dear Marcy. Her heart was too large and soft a target for the world and a boy with a tongue like mine. It was a trick, I said—birds could not live in a box for as long as she claimed. Well that had her crying for sure. Open it, I said.

No, no, not here, she said; it had to be opened at the Indians' graves. She ran with her prize. I followed, over the hill with the river below and sunlight bright on her dress and her hair an envy of every autumn. I heard her call out when she dropped the box and it went tumbling down the hill and I heard the birds in the box screeching and the hiss of the fast dark water.

Marcy Waters kissed me because the moon was pale and wandering and the years had forgotten so much. Her lips were bitter from wild strawberries—like half-formed hearts—that we found coiling and trembling along the ruined boards of old Whitney's fallen barn. We were fifteen summers out of the womb, gangly and white in the darkness, our bodies shivering and brittle-seeming without clothes. I felt the bones through her back and the press of her budding chest against my own hard ribs.

She laughed and lied and I believed her and told her that we were over dead Indians' graves, and that they had killed old Whitney with his own ax and she pretended to believe. Then we lay down like birch branches on the grass.

They all knew the baby was mine—but didn't it look like an owl, feathery-haired, and round-eyed and with strange arms that should have been wings. Marcy never spoke to me after that and they say her father sent her off to live with an aunt in Connecticut, but I saw her sometimes when rain made the river high and the dark waters shaped her face briefly and broke it up again. Maybe her father drowned her there where she used to dream and where she lost the box to the eastward current and cried as the crying birds gurgled. They were the souls of Indians, she said, and they cried for their land and their graves where we raised our corn.

I blame myself now and picture Marcy Waters with her freckles and the quick green of her eyes. In spring I imagine her laughter, and in autumn her grief. I found the box three miles down the river, the wood dark and soft and the latch a blur of rust. I could tell by its weight that it still contained the bones that old Whitney had dug up out of his field and stashed behind his woodpile. I broke it open and waited for the sound of birds, but there was only the sound of a river squirming past the muddy banks and the half-remembered screams of old John Whitney that day that I smeared my face with owl blood, like war-paint, and killed him with his ax.

Whispers

Massachusetts, 1880

Over in Eastborough there stands a handsome brick Georgian house, festooned with ivy and sporting great twin chimneys and long small-paned windows that catch the amber light of a setting February sun. Inside, three wealthy gentlemen sit by a wide flickering fire, their brandy glasses glazed with flame, their voices lowering as if following the sun on its daily course into darkness.

Oliver Welcher is the owner of the house, a retired merchant, previously of Salem. The other two men, one young and curly-haired, with dense red lamb chops hugging his jaw, and the other a weary and stooped older fellow of darker cast, are surgeons. The younger man, Bellows, has just finished telling his ghost story.

"It's your turn, Edmund," the portly host intones, smiling and gesturing with his glass.

Edmund Houghton seems to hunch deeper into his chair, his eyes on the window where the sun has now fallen below a line of pines.

"My life is a ghost story," he mutters, more to himself than anyone else—it is almost an involuntary utterance.

Young Bellows perks. "I'm intrigued!"

Houghton, realizing what has just come from his lips, shifts, grimacing, for his body is capable of few motions that do not elicit some notable degree of pain.

"Well, " Welcher says. "Let's have it."

"I'm sorry," Houghton moves to repair, hiding behind his glass. "Haven't we had enough of wraiths and demons for one sitting?"

Bellows smirks. "Never enough demons. Come now, Edmund, don't tease us."

"My dear friends, I enjoy a good yarn as much as the next fellow, but I really fail to see where my story would amount to a pleasing entertainment. We have had a pleasurable visit this afternoon, and I suggest we leave it at that."

Welcher, being a man of keener sensitivity than the youthful doctor, recognizes the earnest discomfort in his friend's eyes. "Yes, perhaps Edmund is right, another spook tale might be a bit much at this juncture. Perhaps a game of billiards would be the thing . . ."

Bellows frowns. "Edmund can scarcely heft a cigar without agony and you expect him to wield a stick?"

"Better I suffer some aches than you my dreadful little biography."

Bellows creaks forward in his seat and stares. "So you have, in actual fact, seen a ghost, Edmund?"

The older surgeon has his eyes to the window, where the neat square panes are losing their fire and as surely as a sun must set, his words begin to come out.

"Seen, and so much more."

The men settle back *and you should too, safe and comfortable, wherever you are.*

It's been twenty years now . . . I was returning from Reverend

Atwell's house one evening in March, having been called away from my meal to treat one of his sickly children. Lois, I believe.

She had a terrible fever. I had done what I could and was riding home with the darkness coming on and the cold closing in. The road was all mud and the crows were making an awful noise in the woods.

I came around a bend on the road that twists toward Grafton, by the rolling Nourse farmland, and there saw a figure shuffling ahead of me. It was a woman with a frayed black shawl about her shoulders and pulled up over her head, and it was my impression that managing the muddy road was a great effort for her. My mare snorted and this figure looked back over her shoulder. It was Esta Henstick. She was passingly known to me; something of a solitary figure, struggling with the upkeep of her little pig farm following the death of her husband some months earlier. I felt pity for the disheveled creature and offered her a ride.

"My dog has run off," she explained, taking her wrap down, showing her dark hair. "I been searchin' half the day."

"Come now, I'll get you home. It's dark and a dog's likely to make its own way back, don't you think?"

Esta had come close to my horse and looked up at me with her sad little eyes. She was not a pretty thing really and while, I learned later, she was twenty five-years of age, she appeared older, such was the mark of hardship upon her.

Well, to speed the story on, I'll just say that it required some further prompting on my part to convince her to accept my generosity. When she shyly conceded, I dismounted to help her onto my beast, grasping her undernourished waist. Then I climbed up behind her, and we rode on, her dark hair inches from my lips and her shawl against my chest. She was shivering and the moon was moving up out of the trees.

Her house was a sorry little thing set into a low, hill-ringed bit of land, dense with trees and heavy with the smell of her pigs. I helped her down and she seemed ashamed, I want to say, being poor and having a man of my social position and wealth as witness to her squalor. She held her face down and seemed thankful for the dark hair that fell to obscure it.

"Can I repay you in some way?" she said to the earth.

"No, good woman, thank you. It is payment enough to see you safely home."

She turned toward her house then and I saw the heavy sadness in her face take flight and her worrisome small eyes light briefly with girlish glee.

"Bonnie!" she exclaimed, rushing to embrace a rather mournful-looking mutt of mottled colors, which did little to conjure or justify its title.

"You see," said I, "just as I said. Dogs are loyal creatures—they always return home. Goodnight, Mrs. Henstick."

"My name is Esta," she said. "Thank you, sir, and good night."

Well that was that and I was swift on the road toward my comfortable home and my lovely golden-haired wife and my three delightful daughters, each as fetching as my bride.

George Snow had taken quite a blow. A horse's kick had broken a rib on his right side and sent him hard against a fence with the impact. I patched him up and stopped in at Parmenter's Tavern.

Some drinks later, I went out into the brisk dusk and found, close by my horse, a tattered dog of bleak colors.

"Bonnie?"

The dog lifted its bored head and blinked at me.

"She likes you," a voice came from a shadow and I turned to regard Widow Henstick.

I looked back at the dog, which could not have illustrated further disinterest in this storyteller.

"I can see that," I said.

"I recognized your horse," Esta said. "A lovely horse, she is."

I petted my mount on her wide neck. "Earns her keep, I'll give her that."

We stood for an awkward moment and Esta, in her shyness, seemed to be visibly shrinking the whole time, though it was actually the light leaving us and night settling.

"I must be off," I said, swinging up onto my horse.

Esta floated closer, looking up, just then, with a smile that was like those of my daughters when they have drawn something and offer it to me, bristling with timidity and frail emotions, as girls are so thoroughly imbued.

"Good evening," I said, almost curtly.

"Sir?"

I sighed and turned, my patience waning.

"I, I have little, it's true, but I would like for you to have this," she said, and she removed from under her shawl and extended, in offering, a bottle.

"It's some wine. I make it myself . . . each evening I have come here, hoping to make your acquaintance, that I might present it . . ."

"You owe me nothing," I said. "Thank you, but I must be off."

It appeared as if Esta Henstick's face would crumble and I felt a cruel lout. Her chin fell against her shallow chest and she turned in silence and started away.

Memories are whispers and that night in my bed, there were small quiet voices in my secret mind, like ghostly songs recalling the feel of the lonely widow on the horse, against me, for I again carried her to her sullen abode, the wind putting her dark hair in my face and her weight leaning against my ribs and the quickening heart behind them.

I felt obliged, as a man concerned with the healing of wounds, to make some polite gesture to make amends for my harsh treatment of the waif outside the tavern. When we arrived at her shelter, I told her that I would indeed be more than pleased to taste the wine she had been so generous as to offer and further suggested that we share a glass. Well, at that, her face lit as it had before, when she had discovered her dog safe and sound. But just as quickly it went dark and she turned, as if in turning she could entirely hide, or even disappear.

"What is the matter, Esta?" I asked.

"My house is not much to see, sir, and I should be ashamed for a gentleman as you are to set eyes upon it."

"Do not be ashamed. Here, it looks rather cozy from the outside. It can't be less friendly than this chilly evening, at any rate. We'll have a good drink by a good fire and then I'll be off."

I can scarcely account for what followed, but somehow, I found myself in my hostess' arms. She was frail and timid at first, the candlelight warm against her pale flesh, the empty wine bottle wobbling on the close table as the rattling bed bumped against it. Then she was filled with a passion and kissed me with such desperation that the release of her lonely tears was on both of our cheeks. Afterward she clung to me like a child, her breath whispering. I heard it later, deep in my brain as I lay by my faithful Susanna.

How vile I felt, how terribly wretched. I had gone to that woman's house with no intention of placing a hand upon her and yet, somehow, it had happened. The shame was immense and I resolved to spend the rest of my days with the singular purpose of being a worthy husband. Never would I speak to that widow again. Damn her memory, her breathing in my head, playing over and over like some small warm wind, trying to pry open my heart.

Each night I would come home and stand in the darkness above my daughters' beds and pray for their safety, and for their unknowing forgiveness. I would stare at my wife, so much prettier than that dark-eyed woman in the woods.

Slowly, however, my wife became a portrait, a walking portrait. She coiled comfortably in my wealth, so smug and busy making social impressions, so hollow. She was a thing to be envied for the gold on her head, the gold on her finger, my gold in her purse. How had I ever believed that I loved such a woman, when there was Esta, so simple and sweet, like a natural emanation of the shady glen where she spent her modest days?

It was August and the trees were heavy with their leaves and close about Esta's small shadow of a house. We lay upon her bed while thunder pounded the dark above Eastborough, her small face on my chest, breathing.

"Edmund?" She said. "What if there had never been a Susanna... would you have married me?"

I think that I sighed. "Of course," I'd said.

She cried each time I left, like a spoiled child, cried violently. Initially, such displays grabbed and shook my heart, but in time I grew annoyed and her face, all red and squeezed by her grimacing, made me want to slap her. My beloved Esta was becoming pathetic. More and more she asked about Susanna until I began to feel something almost territorially defensive and refused to speak of her. But Esta was insistent, and I came to miss the times when she had seemed softer, more brittle, but she was empowered you see, as women tend to be upon stealing another woman's place by the side of a man, especially a man of wealth.

"Edmund?" she'd ask. "What would Susanna do if she knew? Would she go away?"

I stared at the flame in the oil lamp by the bed. "I don't know," I replied stiffly.

"Perhaps she would take your children and go far, far away..."

I sat up then, moved away from her, and dressed.

The situation became intolerable by the time autumn came. The days went away, wheeling the sun to some cold undisclosed distance and the trees were thinning. Wherever I went I was not free of the dark little widow's voice, hissing in my ear, in my brain, and into my blood. I would close my eyes and see hers, small and sad, staring at me like her foolish dog.

I would walk out of her shabby excuse of a home, tripping on the rocks in her dooryard, hearing her mournful wailing at my departure. It sickened me.

Esta pleaded with me to stay. "Why must you leave me each night to sleep with *her*?" she cried. "You don't need them any longer!"

While I did not wish to look upon her, I whirled about just then and glared. She stood in the doorway of her wretched shack, in her shabby dress, the oil lamp in her hand, her face twisting and contorting—an animated beet!

"I am going home to my family," I snarled. "My wife and my children."

Fury flew into her features then. She waved the lamp about and shouted at me. "You will have no family! I am going to pay a visit to this glorious wife of yours and tell her all! I will tell her, Edmund, and she will hate you and she will go off, far, far away and you will see your precious daughters no more!"

"Damn you!" I cursed and my rage was so great, so sudden and primal, that I reached for the first weapon at hand, that being a good-sized stone at my feet. I hurled the thing with all my force and it struck her squarely in her wide twisting mouth. She dropped with such swiftness that I scarcely witnessed the sudden blood. I went straight to my horse, mounted swiftly and was off, with the sound of her insipid dog howling behind. I did not think of the lamp she had been holding until, a mile or so away, up on the dark twisted road, I turned and saw the flames denoting where her house had been, horrible flames waving through the trees.

How does a man live with such a crime, you may wonder. He simply does. Guilt, pity, remorse, they were all mine in great numbing quantities, but the days move on, the sun comes and goes, the weeks roll forward. My life continued, for I still had my dear children and my wife, a fine home and my practice. In time I may have felt a sense of relief, my tragic indiscretions tucked away behind my consciousness, away from the continuing world.

My name was never spoken in association with Esta Henstick and her unfortunate passing did little to ripple the local waters. Her charred remnants were tucked in the cold ground, the whole of her dingy life tucked out of mind.

Winter fell upon my days, its dreary light turning the world into a gray place. I took comfort in repetition and the familiar distraction of favored beverages and books. I began to harbor softer feelings toward Susanna, perhaps as a function of necessity. Indeed, it was the reassuring sameness that upheld me.

There was a succession of storms in December. Eastborough was stark in snow, the forests that wrapped about the town were like legions of upside-down birds, their terrible claws raking the bleak and windy sky. My girls were delighted and exploited every occasion to play in the abundant white stuff. It gave me some cheer to sit in my study and hear their laughter beyond the frosted window.

One overcast afternoon I sat in my favorite chair half-reading with the sound of their light voices close by. Something near to contentment settled over me and I closed my eyes. I was mere heartbeats from sleep when something thumped at the window. I started and saw a snow-ball flattened against the glass, sliding down, and I heard a chorus of giggles.

I smiled and set my book aside and went to the window.

Voices came through the glass. "Father, look, see what we have made!" they called.

A snowman stood facing me as I peered out, or a snow woman, as the case may be, for the snow had been bunched midway to indicate breasts. The thing stared back with sad little bits of coal and the mouth was one large black chunk. These features might have passed undistressingly were it not for the fact that the girls had balanced one of our oil lamps in the crook of a wide snowy arm.

I marched out of the house and before my daughters' horrified eyes, demolished the thing with my hands, then stood there foolishly in the cold, trembling, without explanation. My youngest child wept and ran to the house.

"What's the meaning of this?" I said, at last. "Why not a conventional snowman?"

The eldest, Julia, explained that the idea had come to her in a dream.

A man of medicine and science has little room for superstition and I dismissed the episode as coincidence. What else could it have been? The following day I brought the girls presents from the doll shop in Worcester.

One night in January, with a light snow falling, I lay in bed by my Susanna. The fire had burned low, its failing light flickering, drowning in a waxing darkness. I listened to my wife's breathing and the breathing wind beyond and a third sound, softer than the others. It came from somewhere within the house and I wondered if the servants were up to some mischief. Someone was whispering outside my bed-chamber door.

I rose stealthily and lit a candle. The voice persisted, but seemed to grow faint, as if moving away. A strange thought came to me, that if sounds were capable of producing temperature, then that was the coldest sound I had ever heard.

There was no one in the dark hall outside my room. A wisp of noise came from farther down. Snowy light from a window there showed a door ajar. My heart shuddered and I became aware of some deep and primitive fear. I grasped at logical explanations, even as I moved toward the room where my daughters slumbered. But they were not asleep, for it must have been their voices that I heard seeping out like a wintry mist. Yes, that had to be it, they were awake and talking.

I reached the door and pushed it open. The two smaller girls were lying on their bed quivering, their eyes open, mouths gasping. Julia was sprawled on her own mattress and a shadowy facsimile of Esta Henstick was standing hunched over her. The apparition had one of its arms stuffed elbow-deep down my daughter's throat.

I shrieked and the horror turned to me, its eyes aflame with great malignancy above a slack black mouth. My two younger girls rasped, then lay still. Julia convulsed, her eyes opened in terror or pain and still I was frozen to the floor, lost in some ghastly dream.

Esta's arm snaked free and she fell flat backward to the floor without a sound. She skated head first across the floor, staring up, wriggling like a fish in a calm stream, crossing the room toward me. I stepped aside and she slithered past, out into the hall.

I rushed to Julia's side and took her hand as her failing nerves gave her one last shake and the life hissed out of her. I heard a scream and raced toward my own chamber.

Esta slid out of the room as before, brushing my legs like a cat as she passed. Susanna was in death throes, gulping at air that could not find her lungs. I cursed and swooned and wept. I took my pistol from under the bed and ran through the house, calling after that demon. From one dark room to the next, I searched and shouted.

At last I collapsed in my study, sobbing, dropping my weapon. Snow was glowing through the window and the pale light came in, vaguely illuminating the figure lying still on the floor, rug-like beside me. I looked down into its hateful eyes and its broken mouth and I lurched up, my back against a wall. Esta lifted up in a queer marionette-like fashion and moved toward me, her arms outstretched and waving like eels. I watched as her hands sank wrist-deep into my chest and I stood there, immobilized, looking into that dead white face. I could feel her icy fingers playing over this and that organ, squeezing them as one testing fruit at market. She pinched and prodded, tracing her sharp fingers around on my lungs, along soft intestines and cupping my maddened heart.

She was gone when I awoke some minutes later. I prayed that it had been a dream, but my family lay dead upstairs. I had been a healthy specimen until that time, but following the dread episode, I was sorely damaged and prone to every ailment. I could, and can to this day, feel the cold that her fingers planted in my body. Twenty years later and I still feel the cold.

The three gentlemen sit in silence. Edmund is exhausted by his telling and stares fixedly at the window where the sunlight is no more than a pink whisper. Bellows is more than quenched and has receded, trembling, into his wing chair. Welcher dabs his eyes with a handkerchief.

The storyteller's friends seem at a loss for words until . . .

Bellows' voice is soft now and he says, "I think I would like another brandy . . . "

Welcher nods enthusiastically. "Yes, yes, another drink. What do you say, dear Edmund, may I get you one as well?"

Edmund is staring out the window.

"She's here."

"What's that?" Welcher asks.

"She's here."

Edmund sees a dark bird flying out of the night, but it is not a bird at all. It is a large hurtling stone that bursts through the window, striking him square in the mouth, like a cannonball.

A Million Dying Leaves

1840

The history books make no reference to the actual fate of Pitcherville, which is not to fault the volumes, for the truth of the matter was never disclosed beyond a certain locality. While I am old now, and my memory betrays me in the short term—often I forget where I've leaned my walking stick or lain my pipe—the events of that autumn are retained with unsettling clarity.

Pitcherville was a modest place, an unexpected little village tucked in dark Massachusetts woods by a lake that was never brighter than slate, no matter how sunny the day. If it were not for the white church steeple poking up from the tree cover, one might have missed the place entirely.

Imbued with Yankee determination, the hundred or so locals lived off the land, the lot of them farmers or herders, with the exception of the blacksmith, an undertaker, the reverend, and myself. I was the village physician.

The nearest town was Charterton, somewhat larger and a half hour's ride south. That autumn there had been an outbreak of consumption there and much of my time was spent in the service of my friend Dr. Benjamin Lamb, who himself had lost a young daughter to the cruel wasting malady.

Those afflicted were placed in quarantine, set away from the town proper in a series of dismal mice-infested shacks. It was my duty to tend them as best as possible. I soon acquired an unforeseen task however, fending off peculiar remedies provided by one of the volunteers who came regularly to aid in the feeding of the patients.

Mrs. Noyes seemed to think that the best thing for the stricken were doses of butter that came from cows that had grazed in the churchyard. Worse yet was the administration of mice (boiled in oil and salt). While there was indeed a considerable supply of ingredients there in the shacks, and while her intentions were good, the old woman was a menace, until she, too, fell ill.

One afternoon I sat by Mrs. Noyes's bed in a shadowy corner and read to her. Acorns could be heard tapping on the roof as they dropped from the venerable oaks that sheltered the place. The poor woman flinched at each impact.

Having degenerated beyond the point where sunlight and fresh air would have any prolonging effect, the feeble woman could do little more than nod and wheeze. Her color was unwholesome and her eyes seemed to be collapsing into her face.

Mrs. Noyes was always a bit on the unusual side, so I took her rare mutterings to be the works of a singular imagination coupled with fever.

"A terrible year," she rasped, "storms in July, drought in August, epidemics come fall . . . "

I paused in my reading, glanced at her, then started again, but she was not finished.

". . . And that wretched burnt man stealing from my woodpile."

This time I placed the book in my lap and studied her. An acorn clattered down the sloped roof above. Lately there had been reports of wood gone missing from stacks and sheds in my own town, Pitcherville.

"A burnt man, you say?" I inquired.

The woman lifted her head from the pillow and hissed, "Well, he *looked* burnt, all dark and gnarled like he was."

Curious, I thought, no one else seemed to have gotten a look at the culprit, but then of course I had to consider the source of this information and apply a measure of skepticism.

At any rate, Mrs. Noyes had nothing more to say on the matter and I read further, until she lay snoring with her eyes half closed.

We buried Mrs. Noyes three days later. It was a brisk October morning, as bright as it was chill, and the leaves were a twirling rain of yellow on Burial Hill. We joked sadly about her remedies.

In the afternoon I rode from Charterton to my home in Pitcherville, where I found my woodpile disturbed. Some of the maple logs had been toppled and others were missing.

"I saw nothing," my Martha insisted, her hair disarranged by the steam of cooking. "But the dogs were barking at *something*."

The mystery would have to wait as my appetite took precedence—the warm smell of a meal was all the more appealing for the cold outside.

In the evening I sat by the fire with a pipe and a book. The wind was in the trees—it hissed in the leaves like the sound of the sea. Several times I rose to peer out at the stacked wood, but I saw nothing out of the ordinary.

The thief was not to return to my property that night, but it seems he was busy elsewhere in the village. On my way to Charterton, come morning, I encountered a neighbor who told me that some of his supply had been purloined.

"My missus heard thumping 'round midnight and saw some fella out the window."

"Anyone we know?" I asked.

"She couldn't really say—he looked to be all in black, or something, just hunched over the woodpile. He was gone by the time I got out there with my gun. Funny thing is my wife said he didn't look to be carrying anything when he headed into the woods, but still there were logs missing."

"Perhaps he noticed her and dropped them before making off," I offered.

"Well, I didn't see any about."

"Perhaps he ate them," I joked.

I was in the midst of delivering a child when news of the terrible events reached me. Lucy Rumford, who served as midwife for Pitcherville, Charterton, Hibbins, and towns beyond, had been felled by the consumption and was off with the others in the isolated shacks, so I was left to mind the mothers.

Ann Southey, a sturdy farm wife with hair the color of a crow, was bringing her third son into the world when the door to the house was shaken by a series of desperate knocks. It was my friend Dr. Lamb together with a team of local Charterton men (some of them armed). Mrs. Southey's oldest boy led the doctor to the upstairs room where the birth was taking place.

"I'm sorry, Joseph," Benjamin Lamb said, removing his hat, "there's something horrible happened in Pitcherville."

I looked up, startled. "Martha?"

"*Everyone*, it seems. They're gone."

"Gone?" I asked. "Where? How?"

"I don't know, Joseph. Everett Brown's boy just returned from there in an awful state. He'd gone to bring a pie to his aunt and said her house was full of leaves and that she was not to be found. Same with every other house he saw—no people, just leaves."

Dr. Lamb offered to relieve me in tending the birth so that I might go with the others, seeing that my wife was among those missing and his family was safe in Charterton. I thanked him and joined the anxious group of men outside.

The first farmhouse we came to was the Fitch place, a modest white thing on a small hill. The house, the outbuildings, and the fields were ringed on three sides by woods that only hours previous had been decked with their brilliant October colors. While there had been no storm, nor even much wind that day, the trees were all bare— bleak, twisted, and gray. Curiously, the downed leaves that one might have expected to see carpeting the earth beneath the trees were nowhere in sight.

Approaching the house, there was a brief moment when it looked as if the front-facing windows were filled with flame, such were the bright colors of leaves filling the rooms, pressing against the glass.

"What in God's name . . ." I muttered.

The men were frightened and moved cautiously up to the door. When opened, it spilled forth a great rasping heap of colorful foliage. It was as if someone had lifted the roof like the lid of a trunk and filled the house with a million dying leaves.

"Hello," they called into the stuffed rooms.

No reply came. A number of us tried to wade into the place, but the leaves were thick from floor to ceiling, and the chambers were full of their dry foresty smell.

Rakes and pitchforks were taken from the barn (where all the livestock was found safe and intact) and we began carving a path through the rooms. Groping through the rustling sea, we encountered furniture buried in place, seemingly undisturbed, and even a cup of half-drunk coffee, hidden on the kitchen table.

A few of the searchers fumbled their way slowly up the staircase, a steady flow of crisp leaves tumbling down in their wake. We heard them shuffling about on the floors above us, and we waited hopefully. They had no good news to share upon returning.

The party of men decided to move on to the next house while I, accompanied by Joshua Brown (the young man who had discovered the leaf infestation while bringing pie to his aunt), took the westerly road toward my home.

The first thing I noticed was that the trees in the vicinity of my house were stripped of their leaves. The second thing I noted was that each of the nine small-paned windows at the front of the house were completely filled with the reds and oranges and golds that had grown upon the maples.

I leapt from my horse and flung open the door. Leaves gushed out and I called into the house. Like the Finch residence, the building was packed with the things. I squirmed my way into the scratchy wall of hissing, rasping leaves, clawing desperately until I was lost in my own home and near suffocated. I found only empty chairs and the hidden pictures on the walls. Crawling on the floors I searched for a body, but there was none to be found. Martha was gone.

Dr. Benjamin Lamb, having finished up with the Southey birth, had arrived with more men from Charterton, come to lend assistance at Pitcherville. I rejoined the mob outside the white church at the common as dusk came cool and dim from the east. There was an air of great agitation and general disbelief at what had been discovered.

Benjamin took me by the arm and led me toward the steps of the peaked white structure, which, like all the other buildings in the village, had been flooded with leaves.

"They found no one, Joseph—not a soul in any of the houses. But they did find *something*, a figure within the leaves; it was roped to a chair in the aisle of the church. There must have been a struggle for there were spent guns, and axes on the floor."

It was at this time that we pushed our way through the bewildered crowd and faced the captive. Even now I am hard pressed to describe the thing that the villagers had managed to restrain, before disappearing. It was like a man in its shape, yet it seemed more tree than human, the exterior surface all gnarled gray bark, the limbs like boughs, the middle like a trunk. But for the horrible dark hole of a mouth, there were no features to be seen.

The prisoner never uttered a sound, but it jerked violently the whole time, as if in convulsion, the chair legs clacking against the granite step of the church. Fortunately the ropes held.

"Look there," Joshua said, pointing, "seems they got a shot off at it."

There was a wound on the torso and several axe marks besides. What showed beneath the bark was the same stuff that one would find under any tree bark—no blood, no muscle, no bone.

Lost to the madness of the whole dreadful episode, I found myself shouting at the thing, "Where is my Martha? What have you done with my wife?"

The creature's round head turned to me, the black mouth staring. There was no answer; the monster simply continued its fits, jerking from side to side, shaking all over.

Someone in the crowd called out, "Kill it!"

"Burn it!" another cried.

The suggestion became a chant. Men scrambled and straw was

gathered—they piled it under and around the chair. I helped them, stuffing armfuls around the blunt hoof-like feet of the thing.

Someone had fashioned a torch and tossed it on the heap; flames swept up around the squirming captive. It rocked violently, painfully, and wood smoke gushed up above it. Still the creature remained silent, though suddenly we heard cries from within the church where there were in fact no people.

Although we had found no living persons in the village houses, no bodies nor even bones, screams came from the surrounding homes, as if the spirits of their occupants were trapped within. It was the same throughout Pitcherville, for at that very moment, when the tree-man went up in flames, all the leaves in all the houses ignited as well.

I did not remain to watch as the monster burned, its body glowing orange, blackening, crumbling to ash. I rode quickly to my house, passing more burning dwellings on the way. There were shrieks like birds in the air and acrid smoke like fog throughout the village. My own home was like the rest, a terrible stark blaze against the purple dusk, the windows filled with actual flame.

I knew my wife's voice well enough to identify her cries. Her agonized screams tormented me until they were drowned out by the roar of the blaze. I tried several times to enter, but the leaves were all alight and swirling in a storm of hot wind within the hall.

Yet she had been gone before the inferno, hadn't she? How could it be that I heard her voice when there was nothing in there but leaves? Only dying leaves.

These many years later I have no better explanation for what took place that autumn of eighteen-forty than I had at the time. I still sit by the fireplace and imagine sounds that no husband should hear.

As for the village of Pitcherville, the books tell only of a tragic fire that burned every house to the ground. It's just as well that the actual events are not committed to print, just as well that the memories are entombed in the minds of a few old men. In some instances, I suppose, the facts are better off forgotten.

Joseph Warren's Invention

ONE

Ever since that day in the shade and summer dampness of his grandmother's garden, Joseph Warren believed there was a dimension of reality that others rarely glimpsed. While the wispy gray hand had appeared only briefly, groping the air before slithering back beneath the clustered mums, it had imprinted deeply upon him, more so than the echoy Sunday morning jargon of the priests. Their stilted renderings of soul and spirit and afterlife paled in comparison to the proof that his own four-year-old eyes had witnessed.

TWO

Joseph, aged forty-seven, slept little now that his young Molly's condition was deteriorating more quickly than he had anticipated. The day and most of the night was spent in his workshop. The few remaining hours of the day he kept vigil by her bed, dozing sporadically. Sometimes he was awakened by her voice and felt fleetingly hopeful, but her words were the work of delirium, as one look at her failing beauty reassured.

The ephemeral ten-year-old machine that housed Molly's soul had become a frightful thing. The typhoid had started as it had with his wife, the flat red spots on her chest, then the fatigue and fever, the glassy eyes and hollowing pallor. If God existed, the man mused, Molly had been a glorious testament to His artistry. But the basic construction was flawed; the human body was too complicated, too frail—Joseph had made his fortune designing more efficient, more permanent devices.

The man bent close to the sleeping girl, a tender hand on the damp gold of her bangs and whispered, "Don't go yet, my dearest, I'm not finished."

A stone-colored sky settled over Grafton and the Blackstone River rushed through the woods, past the brick mills clattering and whirring with the machines Joseph Warren and the other inventors of that age had devised. The world of men was moving faster, driven by a metal heart, the Industrial Revolution well underway—new opportunities for convenience and toil, depending upon one's social position. Trains rattled and hissed across the New England countryside, their smokestacks poking up through the trees like burning top hats. Joseph only half heard as they rumbled by, not far from his house.

The morose face of a boy appeared in one of the workshop windows. Joseph waved angrily.

"Off with you, Franklin!"

His son flinched and was gone. He had been warned many times not to disturb his father, especially now that there was a vital task at hand. Joseph turned back to the table and the strange figure upon it.

Time had betrayed him; he had hoped for the chance to create something more appealing, but Molly was going faster than her mother had, so he was forced to make do. Joseph's creation was a facsimile of the human form comprised of wood and metal, a skeletal thing with an unfinished face. It was his intention to have a skilled craftsman carve and paint his daughter's likeness for the wooden head—there would be time for those details later, but the major elements could not wait.

Determined not to tremble, Joseph inserted a small glass globe into the chest of the thing, between the black iron ribs. His fingers lingered on the glass long after it was fastened and he prayed to whatever would listen.

"You loved me," Franklin said, sitting on the cool grass, a hand on the cool stone that bore his mother's name. "Molly loves me, too, or at least she did; I'm not so certain now; she seems not to recognize me. When she is gone I will have no one."

A crow spoke, a breeze shifted the leaves above and they let out quiet voices. Wildflowers, gathered by the nine-year-old boy, lay wilting.

"Father never cared for me. Now he shoos me away as if I were a dog. He cared only for her. She was his prize. He taunts me, says that she, even in her wasting state, is filled with more life than I have ever exhibited. She was always filled with glee and he showed her off like a painting, but no longer. She's not so pretty anymore."

The trees conversed further—a timid language of wind.

"I think Father is going mad," Franklin said, "Doctor Hawes says as much. He's building a machine to hold Molly's soul, you see. When she . . ."

The boy rubbed his eyes with the back of his hand.

"When she dies, he expects her soul will go into the thing he's making so that she might live forever."

The boy reached down to a deflating posy and picked off a petal.

"I can't imagine someone wanting to live forever, not that she has any say in the matter."

THREE

Late August saw the year nodding toward autumn; the first colors were on the trees and the bracken fanging the edge of the woods behind the house took on a jaundiced hue. Even the house looked weary, though towering and impressive with its steep gabled roof and wraparound porch.

The shadows lingered longer and dusk pressed to the white clapboards as if trying to digest them.

Joseph rushed to light more candles as the dark crept into his workshop, then he made some adjustments to the figure on the increasingly cluttered table that dominated the room. There was a small valve leading into the front of the central globe that, with a switch-mechanism, could be sealed readily when the time came. A flexible copper tube would be fitted to the opening for the actual transference, the opposite end of that shaped into a mask that would fit over Molly's nose and mouth.

The man was desperate now, ever mindful of the possibility that Molly could expire before the project was completed. He no longer resembled himself—a man of power and wealth—and even the servants looked at him as if he were some feral and volatile creature. One night, having worked in the shop past the toll of midnight, he had caught a glimpse of himself in a mirror and been startled by what he saw. Now his distorted image showed in the glass dome that would house his daughter's soul as if he, in miniature, were trapped inside.

There came a familiar knock at the door. It was the walrus-like

Doctor Hawes, his small sympathetic eyes above gravity-tempted spectacles. He entered and nodded a greeting, closing the door behind him.

Joseph glanced up from his work. "Doctor."

"Hello my friend." The doctor regarded the progress, touched the smooth wooden forearm of the thing on the table. "I don't think it will be long now . . ."

Joseph did not respond.

"Joseph, I think you should prepare yourself. This mannequin of yours will not work. You must come to terms with the situation."

"When I was a boy," Joseph said, "I saw a hand—a ghostly thing—rise up from the bed of my grandmother's garden. I have known, since that day, that the body is a mere machine, that the true essence of a person survives—all it needs is another vehicle to occupy."

The doctor sighed. "All right, what if your experiment works, what sort of existence would Molly have? Have you considered that? How will she see without eyes, hear with no ears? How will she communicate?"

Joseph lifted one of the creation's hands, the sharp black metal fingers glinting. "She will write."

"Without eyes?"

Joseph turned and snarled. "I will make her eyes and ears and a voice! Once she is safely in the machine, I will have time to make further modifications. I will not stand by and see her spirit abandoned, like that hand in the garden."

"I'm sorry, Joseph," Doctor Hawes said, backing toward the door. "I'll leave you to your work."

FOUR

Franklin buried the last of the toys in the apple-scented shade of the tree where he and Molly used to sit, when youth seemed an inexhaustible cup and summer ran warm in their blood. He knelt on the upturned earth, amidst the fallen fruit, clasped his dirty hands and prayed for the toys, for wasn't it true that children imbued their playthings with a magic essence derived from their very spirits? This entombing of the toys was a ritual worthy of prayer.

Afterward, Franklin sat on a low branch, legs dangling, hating everything, even the empty air beside him—vast and betraying—where Molly once sat. He could see the distant house and the predatory dusk that crowded around it and the lights in his father's shop. Hours passed until, at last, the windows went black and still Franklin waited. No one came looking for him.

The house was silent and dark when Franklin returned, his small feet barely creaking on the steps that led to the bedchambers. A light flickered gold in the hall and he listened at the door before stealing in.

A single lamp shone weakly and the room was filled with the sound of breathing, damp resonating sounds like drowning wings. Molly lay in her bed, small and pale, her dark mouth open, her hollow eyes themselves like shadowy mouths. Their father was slumped in a chair by the bed, his chin on his chest, his face frightful in its own right, more shadow than flesh. The strange faceless figure of skeletal wood and metal lay beside Molly.

Franklin moved quietly to the bed and found his sister's damp hand. He kissed it and whispered, "Goodbye."

FIVE

Joseph's dream was a succession of memories. Molly, four years old, had wandered away (as was her custom) from the rest of the party picnicking near Hoccomocco Pond in Westborough, where Joseph's brother lived. She bounded down, close to the water, a clump of bread clenched in each hand. The tall black and brown geese intrigued her. She flung a piece of bread and chuckled as two of the birds came waddling. Another bit of bread brought more geese, honking and eager— the others standing by the dark water turned their attention her way.

By the time Joseph reached the girl she was nearly in tears, running away from the twelve or more charging geese. He scooped her up and the birds milled expectantly.

"They mean to eat me!" the girl cried.

Joseph held her tightly to his chest, her rabbit heart racing.

"Nothing will ever harm you," Joseph had assured her.

He saw her again at age six; it was dusk and she was humming, poking in the herb garden with a stick, trying to locate the shooting star that had carved a brief arc of light across the sky. Then there was the time he found her crying by the goat pen—her doll had fallen in and been wrenched apart by the strange-eyed beasts.

He saw her at seven, holding his hand as they watched where the sinking August sun had stained the sky pink above the Grafton hills. He saw her tragic blue eyes as her mother's box was lowered into the earth, felt her small warm hand as she reached up to push his tears away.

A rasping sound jolted Joseph from his dream. He turned to the bed and saw Molly's face. It was white and wide-eyed, the mouth hollow.

"No—wait, Molly, wait!"

Joseph leapt at the bed, grabbed the copper tubing that ran to the globe in the chest of the queer figure beside her, and pressed the mask end over the girl's mouth.

"Please, Molly, please . . ."

He waited a number of minutes, trembling, looking from the girl to his invention and back.

Neither stirred.

"Please."

Joseph worked the switch to close the soul inside the globe, hoping that there was indeed a soul inside. Again he waited, but nothing happened.

"I am too late," Joseph moaned, turning away at last. "I have lost her."

The man covered his face with his hands and sobbed.

Doctor Hawes, who had dozed off in one of the library chairs, was awakened by the sound of the wood and metal creation toppling down the cellar stairs where Joseph had thrown it. He found Joseph standing in the door frame, glaring down into the dark, muttering to himself.

"Joseph?"

The man spoke without turning, "I was too late, Doctor."

"I'm so sorry."

Hawes led the other man into the library and gave him brandy.

"You're certain she's—"

"Go see for yourself," Joseph groaned.

The doctor took up his bag and slipped from the room. Joseph sat staring into the black of the fireplace, numb, only half-hearing the train that rumbled through the close woods. Once the train had passed, the silence returned.

Presently, there came a sound beneath the floor, then quiet, then another sound, like a heavy foot on the wooden steps of the cellar. Joseph sat forward, put down his glass. Another step sounded below.

The man rushed to the basement door and flung it open, staring down into the musty gloom. Was that a faint bluish glow, he wondered, squinting. A distinct thud on the steps.

"Molly?"

He could see it now, his eyes adjusting, the thin figure coming up the stairs, the glossy wood of the arms, the soft gleam of metal ribs and the unfinished face emerging from the blackness.

"It is you, my Molly, it is you!"

A final step brought the figure a mere foot from its creator.

"Molly?"

The figure's arm came up suddenly and Joseph was slapped back against a wall, fiery pressure where the metal hand had struck his chest. The figure moved past him in a rush and made its way to the back door.

"Molly, wait!"

Joseph hurried after the thing, out into the night. He caught a glimpse of it as it moved—a ghastly puppet—away from the house, past his shop, into the woods. Moonlight shone lightly on its thin limbs and there was a soft emanation from the glass ball in its chest.

Doctor Hawes, who was coming down from the dead girl's room when he heard the commotion, now followed out of the house with lantern in hand. He called for Joseph, saw vague movement in the dim maze of trees. He heard the rustling of leaves and a distant hum as a train made its way through the New England night. He huffed along, his lantern's light shifting crazily, the smell of apples on the close air.

He nearly collided with the figure dangling from the apple tree.

"Dear God!"

The doctor staggered back and thrust the lantern up into Franklin's face, saw the blank blue eyes, the tongue, the rope around his neck. He touched the boy's wrist; it was cold—the boy had been dead for some time, longer than the girl.

SIX

Franklin pushed on through the woods, his new, awkward limbs smashing through the foliage. He could see, he could hear, he could feel; he had been cheated of his release! How could it be, he wondered. His body had passed before his sister's, and the boy's longing spirit had been inexplicably drawn to his father's creation, occupying it before Molly's spirit could. Now he could hear his father moving closer from behind and another sound, a rumbling, a clattering, and he shifted toward it, saw the tracks ahead, slick-looking in the moonlight. He would not be deprived of his death.

"Molly, please, wait!"

The thin figure had reached the tracks—it paused, swiveled its blank wooden face toward the closing form of Joseph Warren. The cyclops light of the train was rushing through the dark, making a silhouette of Franklin.

"My dear girl . . ."

Franklin looked back into the light of the roaring train as it traveled closer; he hesitated long enough for the man to encircle him with trembling arms. It had been so long since Franklin had been hugged that part of him wanted to welcome the sensation, but the embrace was not meant for him and he shoved his father away and stepped onto the tracks.

Doctor Hawes burst from the woods in time to see Joseph Warren throw himself at the strange thing standing in the path of the rushing train. Both rescuer and the machine, like some otherworldly upright insect, were met by the steam-gushing black monster, the impact hurling them, its progress uninterrupted.

It took the doctor several minutes to find the bodies. Joseph, flung several yards into the woods, was face down beneath the red-spattered white of a birch trunk. The limbless machine that the man had tried to save was on its back in a bed of ferns, the wooden head split, though the curiously glowing glass bulb had been preserved by the metal ribs.

Doctor Hawes bent over the thing and, after staring for several long moments, reached down to the globe and worked the switch that opened its valve. A misty blue light sighed free and faded into the quiet moonlit air.

Sleep of the Flower God

New England, 1890

When she was young, Constance found herself invoking small gods. They were close in the dark of closed eyes, perched in her internal ether, waiting. When she wanted a new doll, or a pretty dress, when she wanted sunshine, or thunder, she had merely to think them near. All the gods had secret names, but she dare not speak them aloud.

The doll god was clumsy and dull-eyed with weeping-willow hair and a dress that changed color in accordance with the conjurer's disposition. The rain god was a damp gray face at the window. The dress god, or goddess, really, was a shape that swirled under veils and silk.

In May it was the flower god that tickled the night grass with its strange steps. In the morning there were blooms. But Constance caused its death one night in February. A storm of snow had covered the town and the heavy sky had pressed down. How she had longed for spring, lying in her bed with covers across her lips and the dark ceiling hanging above her eyes. She had closed her eyes and filled her head with a warmer darkness and whispers.

Constance had envisioned flowers burning up through the winter crust, defiant colors blurring out of the cold. She saw the small god in her mind, stepping its curious steps, like a dance under water. It looked like an unfed child, but its feet were seeds and its face was a smooth, unfinished sculpture.

Constance fell asleep with the snowy wind brushing her windows and in the morning, when only servants stirred, she dressed and hurried down the stairs. Quietly venturing outside the house, the girl looked at the colorless stretch of land onto which tumbled the last lazy flakes. All was white beneath a potion of milk and ash. No flowers showed.

While many of the birds had long since flown south, there were those that braved the harsh New England winter. Some of these had found something beneath the snow. They fluttered up when Constance approached. She noticed strange almond-shaped impressions in the snow, intermingled with the bird prints, that looked like small broken crosses.

There beneath the snow lay the flower god. Constance had gasped and bent to brush it off. She cradled it and wiped the cold off its smooth green face. The birds had chewed at its limbs, the fingers like the tips of vines.

Inside the house, the dead god lay by the fireplace in her room, wrapped in a shawl. Taking advantage of every offered opportunity, Constance rushed to her room to see if the warmth of the fire had revived the thing. By nightfall, the flower god began to blacken and the room smelled like rotting weeds.

Benjamin enjoyed walking in the hills above the town. It both soothed and inspired him. But there seemed to be so little time to himself since his mother's illness had arrived, just fleeting moments in which to indulge his art. The hills offered some escape and a taste of life as it was meant to be. While picturesque views and natural beauty surrounded him, such things did not always find their way into his sketch book.

The location afforded him an atmosphere conducive to creativity and the creative process was a thing of magic and mystery. An ill-defined impulse stirred a mist inside, a cloud of blurring possibilities in the skull, which, through pencil and hand, took shape. It was as if he were a medium for some otherworldly intelligence to work through.

He drew women who had never walked or breathed and strange spectral places of ethereal beauty. He gave birth to new mythological beasts, gave wing to cherubs and dreams.

That afternoon in May was an exception; he drew precisely what he saw. Two soft hills rose like green breasts. He sat on one and on the other, across from him and unaware, sat a beautiful young woman. She had a parasol and a white dress and loose dark hair and a face loved equally by shadow and sun.

Benjamin conjured the woman in shades of gray, there on her hill, gazing out on the roofs of the town. She was vapor at the start. The lead hissed softly on the paper as he gave her shadows. He made the creases in her skirt and the warm wings of darkness beneath her breasts. She was perfect.

The air grew cooler as the sun dipped down. Benjamin hunched lower over his drawing, detailing her hair and the profile of her mouth. When he looked up again, his subject had risen to her feet and was facing away from him. His heart twisted.

"No," Benjamin whispered. "It's not done!"

The woman floated over the rim of her hill and out of view.

"They say there's a monster up in those hills," Benjamin's mother said, when he told her of his encounter.

Benjamin was robust, handsome as his father had been, with dark curls and serene eyes.

"When I was a girl . . . " the woman's words moved slowly in her mouth, her tongue choosing and sculpting each one with care, "a young couple went to meet there and never came back."

Benjamin sat by the bed, gazing at the incomplete drawing that his mother had refused to view. He chuckled politely. "Mother, that's the very same story you told me as a boy, when I was madly in love with Mr. Mortensen's wife. It frightened me so much that I never set foot on their farm again."

Mrs. Wagner closed her eyes. "There are monsters everywhere."

"You'd rather I didn't return to that place I am so fond of?"

"Did I say as much? You're a young man now, Benjamin. You don't listen to me anyhow. Still, there are other places where you might find peace enough to sketch."

Benjamin flipped his sketch book shut. "I suppose. Perhaps tomorrow, I'll seek a new location."

Mrs. Wagner leaned her bony head back, seemed to shrink into her pillow. "You never were a good liar, Benjamin . . . "

Midway through his waiting, Benjamin refreshed himself with the wine and cheese he had brought in a hamper. There was no sign of the lovely young woman. Her hill stood grassy and steep, with a dark pucker of clouds rising up behind it, as if the village below were burning. The thunder, distant at first, stepped closer in great hollow boots. The clouds spread out and rain tiptoed in the grass around him.

Benjamin gathered up his art supplies and hamper and hurried down the hill to where the edging forest offered shelter. Shadowy leaves jerked beneath the heavy drops. He ducked beneath the trees as the shower filled the air and found himself face to face with the woman he had drawn the previous afternoon.

"Hello," Constance said. A raindrop stole through the cover, skimmed her cheek, and rolled over her lips.

"Hello," Benjamin breathed.

The young woman held a sketch pad. "I hope you don't mind," she said, smiling shyly, holding out her drawing.

The picture showed the hill, as seen from the bordering wood below, with Benjamin sitting on top gazing off to the west.

"Why no," Benjamin's face pinkened. "I'm flattered that you found me a worthy subject. And it's such fine work, but who is that woman standing behind me?"

"I don't know."

"I was under the impression that I was alone."

"You were, really, I only saw her in my mind."

Benjamin smiled.

The woman in the picture was familiar.

"I, too, come here to sketch. May I show you one?"

Constance took a small step closer. It was dark beneath the trees and the rain hummed and slapped on the leaves.

Benjamin flipped through his pictures until he came to the most recent. Constance saw his face change.

"Mother!" he hissed.

"A picture of your mother," Constance said, leaning closer, "how nice that you sketch your mother."

Benjamin tore the page out and crumpled it before Constance could see. Apologetically, he explained, "I'm afraid I'm not pleased with it, after all."

She must have done it when he slept, he thought, dragged herself from her sick bed and drew herself into his picture of the girl on the hill, drew herself hovering menacingly with her bony hands outstretched to the back of the girl's neck.

Benjamin did not invite Constance to the house until after his mother's funeral. The women never did meet, and Benjamin had kept their afternoon meetings a secret. But love found their hearts there on the warm green hills and wildflowers sang their scent into the air.

"When I was a girl," Constance said, standing in his bedchamber, unbuttoning her dress, "I conjured my own little gods."

Benjamin saw her breasts for the first time, soft in the afternoon sun.

"One winter, I called on the flower god, but it was too cold and he died in the snow."

The dress slid down away from her plush dimpled belly, down over her fine, wide hips, then her thighs.

"I kept him for days, but he began to rot."

Constance stood naked.

"I buried him in the yard and the grass turned brown, but the following year there was this great cluster of spring flowers. It terrified me so, but it was beautiful, too, how its sleep became the soil. I think of my own skin going back to the earth one day, and it exhilarates me."

Constance moved her hands over the rounded warmth of her flesh. She lifted her heavy breasts up, kneading and shaping, as if working dough. She tugged at the ends until they were strawberries, hard with aching blood.

Benjamin was trembling and crying when he returned with the bucket of mud.

"Mother was lying in the stream! I saw her in the dark water, staring up at me!"

Constance held him and reassured him. "It was nothing, my love, only your grief making a shadow in the water, and nothing more."

She took his hand and dipped it in the warm mud, then pressed it to her chest. The hand slid down, drawing a dark glistening blur. His finger made a small moist sound as it slipped in then out of her navel.

She looked like the dead flower god lying on the bed with a batter of damp earth encasing her. She had caked it thickly on her face so that her features were only smooth impressions. Benjamin drew her like that and, at her insistence, entitled it: "Sleep of the Flower God."

Then he climbed on the bed and onto her and she was slippery brown and gasping beneath him.

The bath water seemed gold from the candles, and Constance lay back in the heat and steam, her eyes shut, her body clean. It was late and the crickets outside shared rumors of the coming frost. She listened to them and to her own breathing. She felt her heart as it counted softly within. She felt the crowding of cold legs in the water with her and her eyes opened.

Mrs. Wagner was slumped at the opposite end of the tub, bony and naked, her rictus mouth all horrible teeth and her eyes glaring in dead malignance.

Constance did not scream. She closed her eyes and called to the warm dark. With her own voice inside her head, she whispered the name of the god of stones. She saw him shuffle up out of the dark, gray and strong, and she told him to go to a grave, told him to fill the coffin with stones to weigh the occupant down.

When Constance opened her eyes, Mrs. Wagner was gone, never to be seen again.

The Puppet and the Train

Massachusetts, 1909

Although there were several known cases of human infestation, actinomycosis, more commonly known as lumpy jaw, preferred cattle by a notable margin. The insidious little fungus stole into the body of an animal, more often than not the head, where it inspired swelling and created an abscess within the inflamed area. Gabriel Burkett had seen untreated animals afflicted with tumors the size of coconuts.

Even when kneeling, Gabe seemed tall. He was down in the shadow of a barn, long gentle fingers moving over the jaw of a hulking milk cow. The animal shifted nervously, moved its large eye, and snorted. The veterinarian leaned his face close to its head and whispered soothingly.

Joseph McDonald, the cow's owner, stood watching with his hands in his pockets. He had seen Gabe at work before, observed his solemn precision, and he trusted the veterinarian implicitly.

Still kneeling, Gabe nodded to himself, thought a moment more and looked up. "It's lumpy jaw, all right," he said. "If we had caught it sooner, I'd have cut it out, but it might be into bone at this point and there are some good-sized blood vessels to consider."

Gabe felt around some more, then stood. He patted the beast's great neck.

"Simple enough, " Gabe concluded, "we'll give her iodide of potash in her drinking water for a week or so. That should do nicely."

McDonald grinned. He was expecting something more invasive, something more complicated. Gabe looked him in the eye, like a preacher would, and while a younger man at forty-six, he spoke in a fatherly fashion, "Now Joseph, if you should happen to notice this sort of thing again, don't wait so long to fetch me, all right?"

McDonald nodded. "I won't, Gabe, I won't."

The men stepped away from the barn into the warm June sun. They turned to the road, alerted by the sound of a motorcar's horn. A Model T raced around the bend and came to a dusty stop. Gabe frowned. He hated "Tin Lizzies" and relied on his beloved horse for transportation. Mankind, he felt, was not wise enough to responsibly wield the power of its technology. Bombs, guns, and soaring horseless vehicles demonstrated his point menacingly, succinctly.

Young Dan Muir, son of a lawyer and a neighbor of the two men, sprang from the automobile, goggled and wind-haired. He seemed breathless, as if he had run the length of dirt road to the McDonald farm, rather than driven it in his expensive metal contraption.

"Doctor Burkett," the man called, "you must come—there's been a terrible accident down where they're setting up the circus in Gaughan's field."

Gabe threw McDonald a woeful look before climbing reluctantly into the sputtering machine.

They raced over the top of a hill and drove down to where a

stretch of railroad tracks gleamed out from behind a dense wall of small trees and tall bushes. Gabe cursed quietly to himself. He thought the accident scene looked like a cross between a children's book illustration and a nightmare. A train had plowed into the side of an elephant.

Poor jousting partners, a locomotive and an elephant. The giant gray mammal, like some misplaced corporeal relic of prehistory, was on its side; the steaming black metal monster had simply tilted off its rails. There was a great dark wound on the side where the tusked beast had taken the blow. The man who had been leading the elephant across the tracks when the train came roaring out of the bushes had fared the worst. No need to check for a pulse there. Strangely, there was more blood from him than from the larger animal.

A small crowd had gathered; the motorcar stopped. Burkett could only stare until Dan Muir turned to him and said, "Can you help it? See there, the front legs are kicking; it's still alive!"

"I've never treated an elephant," Gabe muttered.

"But you're a veterinarian; you can help it, can't you?"

Gabe did not reply. He took up his bag, climbed out of the car, and pushed his way through the crowd.

It was an Indian elephant, that much he knew. He could tell from the tusks, smaller and straighter than those of the larger African breed. There was an unpleasant burnt smell close to the creature. He leaned over the massive wrinkled head and gazed into the black eye, big as a fist. The eye did not seem to contain anything like a spark of life, yet a thick, dry trunk coiled around Gabe's leg and quivered. Startled, Gabe took a step back, nearly tripping over the appendage, which went limp following its tremor. Perhaps it was an involuntary nervous reaction; he had seen animals move in curious ways at the point of death and shortly thereafter.

The elephant was cold to the touch, cooler than the air, as if it had been dead for some time, though the accident had happened just a quarter of an hour previous. Gabe put a hand in front of the mouth and felt no breath. He worked his way back. Its side was not moving; there was no evidence of breathing whatsoever. The front limbs had stopped the spastic motion he had observed from the car, looking down as they came over the top of the hill, looking out over the colorful spired circus tents with their stripes and flags and the clutter of wagons like an encampment of gypsies.

"Look there!" someone in the crowd called out suddenly, and Gabe turned, looking up as a thin, naked man with brownish skin pulled himself up out of the enormous, surprisingly bloodless wound in the elephant's side. The man had wild black hair and wild black eyes and threw the crowd a glance both feral and contemptuous before springing from the dead elephant and racing off into the thick greenery nearby.

"Dear God," Gabe hissed.

"Catch him," the shout went up, and after a baffled pause, some young men did charge off in pursuit.

Gabe climbed up the body and peered into the wound, through the pale bars of the elephant's ribs into a hollow space where one would have expected to find an assortment of organs. It was like a room, the roof darkened as if a fire had been lit inside, and there was a dry tree bark-colored floor. Gabe reached a trembling hand down into the thing and scooped up two pale objects which appeared to be candles, slipping them into his pocket.

Below, a man with a pointed beard of silver, sporting the long coat and the tall hat of a circus master, was bemoaning the loss of Trevor the Talking Elephant. He seemed less concerned with the trainer, whose segments now lay beneath a pair of damp blankets.

Dizzy, Gabe sat on one of the mighty gray legs, as if on a bench, and stared at the earth. He heard the rushing hiss of steam from the big black engine and watched as an ant dragged off a small piece of the elephant trainer.

We find Gabriel Burkett at his humble home that overlooks an orchard in the southern hills of a small central-Massachusetts town. Tired from interviewing members of the circus, the driver of the train, and having discussed the bizarre situation with the local police, he only let his wife Audrey hear the more mundane aspects of the case. He did not wish to disturb her with the whole story for even he, a man accustomed to seeing sad and distressing sights, was himself unnerved by that afternoon's events.

The days in June were long and they sat outside after eating and watched the sky over the town as it went to orange and pink and deep, blue. Roofs and steeples poked up through the distant billowing green of trees. Gabe thought about the thin brown figure that had dashed into the brush. The men who had gone looking for him had not been successful.

Though a serious-looking man, Gabe did not appear stern. He had dark, somewhat wavy hair and dark, deep-set eyes. There was something melancholic about his face, the features both intense and gentle. A child had once told him that he looked more like an undertaker than a veterinarian. He gazed over at his wife, who sat on the farmer's porch with him, her lap a tangle of knitting, and he made a mental note to himself that he should (uncharacteristically) lock the door that night.

Lying in bed, he thought about the train, like a great metal puppet caterpillar, racing along with men inside, and wondered if—though it seemed impossible—the elephant had served a similar purpose, transporting its lone passenger, or, more accurately, its pilot. It had to have been dead before the train hit it; no animal can live with the majority of its vital organs missing. And where had those gone? The train had ripped the wound in the thing's side and, having inspected the carcass, Gabe had found no scars to indicate an earlier extraction of the poor behemoth's innards.

Unable to sleep, he quietly rose and bent over the bed to touch Audrey's cheek. Sometimes she spoke out in the darkness, especially when their large amber and white cat moved restlessly, repositioning himself to find the most comfortable spot, thus disturbing her. She would mutter from a place between sleep and the world. She did this now. "Crouching on a roof...black mist from the lips," she said, then settled back into soft rhythmic breathing. Her husband brushed a strand of cidery hair from her face.

Gabe walked downstairs and found the two candles in the pocket where he had left them. He had not told anyone else about them, none of the other stupefied townsfolk, not even the police. In a way he was afraid to have others see them, for it would make it harder to deny that such a mystery could exist in the world if there were more than one witness.

One of the resident circus freaks, a woman from Mexico who was covered in long dark hair, had told Gabe that she had heard strange noises one night and had wandered out of her tent to see a strange brown woman inserting a small cloth doll, like a witch's poppet, into the birthing place of Trevor the Talking elephant. The elephant was known as Bessie then and performed in a ring and was also made to move heavy objects. That was before they discovered that the elephant could talk, and it was only later that the name was changed to Trevor. Somehow the circus proprietor seemed taken with that bit of alliteration and felt that the public would respond better to a talking male elephant more so than they would a female. Besides, the creature spoke in a masculine voice.

Gabe sat for a time just holding the candles. They had a strange feel, as if they were made from pale flesh, and they smelled of rare and secretive herbs, from far off lands where a New Englander ought not venture. When at last he lit one, and saw the bizarre images in the light around the flame, he blew it out and hid both candles away in his desk.

One might think that an enigmatically hollowed-out elephant would make for a fine sideshow attraction in a circus. It was not to be. For while the curious flocked, the owner of the traveling entertainment had ordered the burning of the body mere hours after its demise. Gabriel Burkett learned this the next day, when he returned in hopes of better examining the creature. What veterinarian or man of science could blame him for wanting to? He was sorely disappointed to find that the remains had been destroyed. As for the circus, it packed up and left in the middle of the night, days earlier than scheduled. Those seeking thrills and diversion found only a trampled field.

Windy pines framed the pasture where Gabe knelt by a sheep in sunny grass. A farmer and his sons hovered nearby and Gabe's horse was grazing. Idyllic as the sprawling farmland appeared, it was haunted by tiny monsters, such as those that had caused the blindness in the patient Gabe was examining.

Felix Griffin had summoned Gabe because the sheep had taken to walking in circles and seemed incapable of straight, forward motion. Then its vision went.

Gabe stood above the others when he rose, wiping his hands on his trousers. His face was grim and his voice low, "It's not good, Felix. I believe it's a case of gid in sheep. Are you familiar with it?"

"No," the farmer said.

"Occasionally a sheep will ingest the eggs of a bladder worm—a tapeworm in an early stage, actually. Well, the eggs hatch in the stomach and the worm gets into the blood and lands up somewhere else in the body, maybe the lungs or the heart, or in this case, the brain." Gabe pointed to his own skull.

Absently stroking the back of the sheep, the doctor continued. "This walking in circles indicates that only one side is infected. The blindness is another indication of bladder worm. The condition is advanced enough for me to feel some softening of the skull."

The farmer was staring at the animal, nodding as he listened.

One of Griffin's freckled boys looked up at Gabe and asked, "Are you going to kill her?"

Gabe crouched down to face the boy. "This poor beast is very ill, son. Sometimes we have to put an animal down as an act of mercy, or to prevent it from spreading a condition to other animals."

"But this one is my favorite—"

"Your favorite, you say? Well then, maybe I'll try something. There's nothing to lose, really. But will you promise you won't hate me if I can't save her?"

"I promise," the boy said.

The sheep was moved back to the barn and prepared. Gabe located the soft spot on its skull and went to work with a trocar and cannula. He used a syringe to draw the filling out of the cyst.

Following the procedure, Gabe and the farmer stood outside in the tilted afternoon light.

"What do you think, Doc?"

Gabe sighed. "Well, there is a risk of brain inflammation, and that could be fatal, as one might expect. There could even be another worm in there that I didn't get. I can't be certain. We'll hope for the best."

The young freckled boy came up to Gabe and shook his hand. "She's going to be fine, now, I know she is. Thank you, mister."

Gabe always looked both sad and hopeful when he smiled.

The tempo of Aileen McCutcheon's humming was usually dictated by the particular task she was involved with at any given time. There were slow wistful airs when she knelt weeding in a warm garden of summer herbs. Jaunty reels accompanied the husking of corn, a ritual performed in a creaking rocking chair beneath her favorite maple. Patching her husband's wounded farm clothes called for slow quiet tones and now, in the kitchen, hustling to get a meal on the table, a swiftly melodic country dance tune swirled with the smells and steam of cooking.

The chickens sounded outside. There was always the risk of foxes and occasionally a neighbor's dog, or even a group of dogs, would steal into the yard and wreak havoc. Aileen glanced out the window into the yard and gasped.

A naked man with brownish skin and tousled black hair was crouched over a dead rooster. The other chickens lay convulsing on the ground around him. Aileen screamed and the stranger lifted his head to look at the window. He smiled menacingly, his wild eyes agleam and wispy black mist hissed out between his teeth.

Aileen released a series of piercing shrieks that sent the man running and brought her husband and his brother from a close field. They found her standing in the yard with the dead birds.

Gabriel Burkett stood holding the rooster, absently stroking its dead feathers. He studied Aileen intensely, nodding along with her words as she pointed to the grassy hill behind the farmhouse, describing how the lithe brown man had sprung away like a startled deer.

Ronald McCutcheon had taken a rifle and gone over the hill behind the house, searching the edge of the woods that blurred to green and black shadows, while Ronald's brother had gone to fetch the veterinarian and Edgar Gould, the chief of police.

"Sounds like that fellow from the circus," the chief said.

Gabe nodded; the thought had occurred to him, too. He set the rooster down and bent to examine a hen.

The chief was tall, with silvery hair and spectacles. He turned a slow circle, squinting. A search of the farm buildings had been fruitless. He watched Gabe for a moment. It was unusual for him to see the animal doctor in a state of puzzlement.

"Did he break their necks?" the Chief asked.

"No. No signs of violence whatsoever," Gabe reported.

"What do you make of that black on the beaks? Looks like carbon from a fire."

There was a strange burnt smell in the air.

"So it does," Gabe agreed.

Ronald McCutcheon poked at one of the birds with his boot. "So, you don't know how he killed them?"

Gabe shook his head. "I suggest you don't eat any of them, Ronald. He may have used some kind of poison. I'd like to take one with me to do a postmortem."

"A what?"

"An examination."

"Oh. Of course," Ronald said.

"Well," the Chief said, "let me know if you find anything, Gabe. I'm goin' home—all these dead birds are makin' me hungry."

"Don't stay up too late," Audrey said. She kissed Gabe's forehead and went upstairs to bed.

When he finished with the chicken, the man moved from his examination room with its silvery tools and tables, its jars and bottles and sharp chemical smells. He settled in the modest library that looked out on moon-haunted pines. The two candles he had taken from inside the elephant were still hidden in the desk. He wondered if they would tell him more than the body of the bird had.

The examination had mystified Gabe. The hen appeared normal but for two things: the dark scorch-like black on the beak, and the heart, which was brittle and shriveled, like a dried prune.

Following a moment of hesitation, Gabe lit one of the stout fleshy candles. He folded his arms tight against his chest, but a chill found him through his clothes. Soft images blurred out of the hazy nimbus around the flame. It was as if he were in a moving vehicle, watching through a watery window.

There were familiar fields and houses. Familiar roads. At one point he seemed to be witnessing a view from a neighbor's roof, then he was crossing the dark slow waters of the Assabet River, where he had played as a boy. It was night and the visions came like living paintings, traveling north. Through Northborough, the western corner of Marlborough, into Berlin. A house loomed, a dark window close, then inside, up some stairs. A door opened. It was a closet. Clothing hung in darkness. Then the first candle burned out and the air smelled scorched.

Trembling, Gabe lit the second candle, and its ghastly glow was full of ghostly motion. Outside the house in Berlin a sweet-faced old dog looked up, then sagged to the ground. Moon-suggested roads passed. A raccoon; it fell over on the earth, kicked, lay still.

The candle was shrinking. There were only fields and woods now.

"Landmarks," Gabe whispered urgently, "show some landmarks!"

The candle was sputtering. The pictures in the air above his desk grew dim and faded.

"Damn!" Gabe pounded the desk. The images had only shown him the direction, not the destination.

There was a trail of dead animals, like breadcrumbs, scattered from Eastborough to Berlin. Dead cows, dead wildlife, dead pets. Gabe's heart ached. He saw the faces of farmers, their eyes dark with woe as they observed fallen flocks, the wet eyes of children cradling limp kittens and loyal sightlessly staring hounds. Brooding with a thin old man in a pasture where sheep lay crumpled like shrapnel from an exploded cloud, Gabe turned to the fellow and asked, "Is there a gunsmith in this town?"

The Browning 1903 was a small, simple automatic. It was comfortable in the hand and flat for easy concealment in a pocket or a waistband. Gabe hated guns. Gabe handed the gunsmith some bills and turned to leave. A box of bullets and the weapon added alien weight to his coat. He pushed the door open and the bell on it jingled.

It was bright outside and he moved to his horse, Sarah, who was tied outside. He stepped around to her left and came face to face with the thin brownish man he had seen climb out of the dead elephant.

The man smiled. He was dressed in fine clothes and his hair was combed back, tame. He was handsome, charming in the way he carried himself, some might think.

"Hunting does not suit you, Doctor," the man said, his face too close. His breath had a burnt smell. "Shouldn't you be off helping some crippled duck or something?"

Gabe could not locate his voice at first.

The man reached up and stroked Sarah's warm brown neck.

"What are you?" Gabe's voice quavered.

"A puppet," the man said cheerily, "just like you. We're all puppets to our natures. Unfortunately *our* natures seem to be at odds. You're good at helping creatures, and I . . . "

The man turned so that his mouth was several inches from the horse's snout and he exhaled a burst of black mist. Sarah gasped and collapsed sideways, her great weight thumping dead on the dusty street.

"No!" Gabe cried.

The brown man grinned, turned, and darted away. Gabe fumbled his weapon out, tried to remember how to remove the clip from the bottom of the handle, finally managed that and, with quaking hands, attempted to slip bullets into the magazine, the way the gunsmith had shown him.

It was too late. The man had pranced like an antelope down Berlin's main street, past the big brick bank, the pale stone library, and the shops with great gleaming windows, and was gone. Gabe dropped the gun and knelt by his horse in the road, running his hand over her face as tears ran down his own.

Summer passed and September came, the days growing cooler as the frost moved downward from Canada—slow and steady steps of ice. The days ever shorter, afternoon balanced on a quiet sense of expectation, and a growing sense of resignation.

Gabe had returned to a world of normalcy. For weeks he had gone into the woods to practice shooting with the small pistol, telling Audrey he was going for walks. He had gotten quite accurate, but now the gun sat in a drawer in his desk, in the library.

He no longer brooded over maps, speculating on where his enemy might have gone, or might be headed. The trail had ended in Concord. Some dairy cows had died mysteriously, he had heard, and their faces had born the telltale scorching. But that was the last incident; there were no more reports of strange animal deaths. Perhaps it was for the best, he thought. That monster could probably have dropped him just as easily as it had dropped Sarah. It was a powerful opponent, and likely imbued with uncanny sensitivities, for it had recognized Gabe and even appeared to know his intentions.

Life seemed right, sitting there on the porch with his Audrey, watching the sky go from orange to pink to cool September blue; she with her knitting and soft graying hair, the loose strands from her bun giving her a girlish look. Gabe looked out over the trees and knew there was a vast world out there, with great bustling cities, and exotic countries, each with their own marvels and charms, but he loved the simple things and the familiar. He did not hunger to roam and explore. The hills and fields, the old homes and stone walls, the orchards and woods of the town he loved were enough for him.

Gabe gazed over at Audrey as she rocked, humming. He smiled, and his smile was both hopeful and sad.

"Motorcars," Gabe muttered disdainfully, hunched over the injured pig.

Sam Maynard, the farmer, paced in the dirt, cursing beneath his breath. His twelve-year-old son, who had been learning to drive their year-old Indiana-made Black Crow, stood guiltily near, pouting.

The animal was well-behaved, under the circumstances. It lay on its side breathing nervously, kicked a bit at first, but did not struggle or try to escape. Gabe spoke to it in a comforting whisper as he worked, checking the injured leg for broken bones, of which, fortunately, there were none.

At last the veterinarian looked up. "It might have been much worse, I should say. No breaks. The wound is not so bad; no need for stitches."

Maynard was relieved and smiled. "She made such a sound when he hit her—scared the Devil out of me!"

"That's because she was scared more than hurt, I'd be willing to say," Gabe ventured. Treatment was simple enough. He cleaned the wound and dusted it with powdered iodoform before bandaging.

Gabe rose, tall and straight, and clapped his hands together. He checked his pocket watch, slipped it back into his vest. "She'll be fine, Sam, just keep her out of the mud until that heals over."

The farmer barked at his son," Get her into the hog house and clean yourself up for supper."

Turning to the doctor, the man spoke more softly, "You're welcome to stay and have a bite, Gabe. The missus is baking a chicken."

"You're kind to offer, Sam, but my missus is, too, and she's queen of the world when it comes to baked chicken." Gabe chuckled. "I best be off."

Sam walked Gabe to his new horse, Nipmuck. The tall man mounted and before heading off, asked, "Say, Sam, how's that prized hog of yours doing? Did that ginger clear up the indigestion?"

"It sure did, just like you said. In fact, we're taking her up to Derry, New Hampshire, come Saturday—there's a big fair up there, you know. You might want to take your Audrey up for the day; have yourself a good time. I hear there's to be an apple-pie contest and an ox pull and even a talking cow, if you can believe a thing like that."

"A talking cow?"

"That's what they say." Sam chortled.

Gabe shivered. "Well, Sam, feels like it's going to be a cold night. I better be on my way."

"A hundred dollars?" Dan Muir exclaimed. "Well sure, Doc, I'll drive you. Hell, I'll drive you to Timbuktu for a hundred dollars."

"Excellent," Gabe said stiffly. He left McTaggart's Pub, where he had known he'd find young Muir, and rode swiftly to his cozy home, which somehow felt warmer, filled with the smell of baked chicken. But Gabe's appetite had been compromised, and he could do little more than dream into the steam wisping up from his plate.

In the morning, after slipping into his library and fumbling in the desk, he told Audrey that he was going for a walk, to take in the changing foliage in the woods.

Muir came by the house shortly after nine o'clock and tooted his horn. Gabe thought the Model T looked like a cross between a coffin and an insect, black and gleaming in the September sunlight.

"Ready, Doc?" Dan Muir called.

Halfway between his porch and the idling metal monstrosity, Gabe turned and gazed back at Audrey, who stood smiling unsuspectingly. He wanted to have a good long look at her, in case it was his last.

Over roads of gravel and dirt, roads soft with mud and crisp with leaves, they traveled north. On through Middlesex County, through the city of Lowell, with its great brick mills churning, up into Collinsville, with green pastures, golden haystacks, and rustling acres of corn. They crossed into New Hampshire, and the road was a lonely ribbon of brown through dark pine forest. Hawks hung like kites in the clear sky and hills of blue haze rose up.

Small villages passed, white churches looming brightly against changing maples and ragged spires of fir. Gabe, quiet and too distracted to focus on his own fear of traveling in the Ford, grinned when they came upon one of those motorized buggies, commonly called high-wheelers, stuck in the muddy road. Popular with farmers and built to negotiate such rural routes, the buggy's thin wheels were no match for the deep dark puddle that dominated a low point in the path. The farmer had hitched a massive draft horse to his technological wonder. Gabe chuckled bitterly when the horse pulled the buggy free.

"All of these contraptions would be better off with horses pulling them," Gabe declared.

"Don't blame the machine," Muir said. "It's the driver's shortcomings that got him stuck." He maneuvered the Model T onto the grassy bank of the road, around the puddle and the embarrassed farmer, and sped onward.

Dan Muir gave Gabe a funny look when the veterinarian handed him the hundred dollars upon arriving at the county fair in Derry.

"You needn't pay me now, Doc. I figured you'd wait 'til we got home."

Gabe shrugged ambiguously and set off through the crowds.

There were tents and the smell of cooking, close laughter and great-eyed children. Gabe craned his neck, searching. His pulse was fast and dizziness rose swiftly to his head along the road from his heart. He reached into the pocket of his gray coat and clung to the cold metal there.

There was a large wooden structure erected for the occasion; a long steep roof supported only by beams. Much of the activity was centered there. Gabe worked his way over, excusing himself politely, numbly, as he stepped closer, moving through the throng. It was shaded and cool beneath the roof and there were tables and more milling bodies. Prize-winning pumpkins, prize-winning apples, prize-winning grain were all on display. He could smell the corn, gold, pale, and sweet.

There were household goods made by women and a section where men, with thumbs crooked in their suspenders, gazed eagerly upon newfangled labor-saving farm devices. Gabe moved along, floated tall in the crowd, the hum of his blood moving faster.

Exiting one of the mall's far ends, Gabe studied the field where the fair had been set up. He could see the rail pens with their show-beasts enclosed. Closer still and he could smell the warm earthy animal smells. Bored and nervous creatures paced, chewed, or impossibly tried to become invisible, tucking themselves into hay or corners in their tight pens. There were ribbons tacked to the enclosures—best ewe, best heifer, best bull. Cows lowed. But where was the talking cow?

More tents stood ahead, beyond the livestock area. There was a touch of carnival atmosphere. A garish painting of a two-headed lamb loomed up. People had gathered around for a contest to award $2.00 to the woman with the smallest feet. A larger group stood outside a pale rippling tent from which came the scent of fresh hay and manure. Gabe saw the sign with big red letters, heard a boy out front, like a barker, calling, "Come see the magnificent talking cow! Come one and all and view this miraculous wonder. Hear it speak and answer your questions!"

Gabe stared at the crude painting of a black and white cow as people bumped against him, pushing past to join the human herd. He found himself in line, moving slowly toward the freckled boy, felt the money leave his hand.

It was dark inside and a man with a bushy white beard was addressing the group, which faced the dully staring cow. The animal stood in a tiny pen up on a pedestal at the center of the enclosure. The beast looked innocuous enough.

The farmer, dressed handsomely in an expensive suit, thanks to his freak cow, chose from a small sea of raised hands; everyone wanted to ask the talking cow a question. "You there," the man said, pointing to a pretty young woman.

"What's your name?" the girl giggled, feeling rather foolish.

"Betsy," the cow replied in a voice that sounded rather masculine for a Betsy.

A low murmur went through the crowd.

The farmer gave a big toothless smile. "Someone else?"

Again the hands went up and the farmer, gloating like a ring-master, pointed to Gabe, tall, solemn looking, with dark, deep-set eyes. Gabe edged closer. He strained to see the side of the cow, which bore strange markings, as if the hide had been opened and then melted shut.

Gabe was about to speak when a familiar voice assaulted him. "Hey, Gabe!"

It was Sam Maynard. He and his son stood nearby, and the farmer thrust out a blue ribbon that his pig had won.

"Look, Gabe, we got first prize!"

The sideshow's host sounded impatient now. "You had a question, mister?"

Gabe's concentration had been broken by the appearance of his neighbor. He turned back to the cow's head, large and close through the bars of its pen, and his hand slid back into the gun pocket. He felt the weight, the trigger, the sweat and heat in his palm.

"Yes, I have a question. Tell me, Betsy, how is it you can talk?"

The cow raised its skull to the man and the mouth moved and, looking into its eyes, Gabe could tell that the animal was not truly alive—not in the conventional sense.

The beast answered evenly, "My speech is a gift from God," it said.

Gabe edged closer still, in the cramped, choking shadows of the tent. "What god might that be?"

"The very same god that gave you speech," the cow said.

His hand came up, and the gun banged and flashed, again and again. The tent filled with smoke and noise. People screamed and stampeded to get out as Gabe fired into the head and body until the gun was empty and clicking. The cow shrieked as a man would shriek and toppled heavily onto its side.

"Son of a bitch!" the beast's owner cursed, rushing at Gabe.

Gabe spun to face the man, said, "It's a monster! A monster!"

The farmer struck Gabe in the face and he went down, dropping a crescent-bladed pruning knife he had pulled from his coat. Others, seeing that he was out of bullets, converged, kicking him. He looked up, saw Sam Maynard staring in horror and confusion.

Gabe called to him, "Sam, cut it open! The right side—cut it!"

Gabe curled on the ground as a flurry of feet thudded against him. He gasped and coughed. Sam hesitated for a moment, then grabbed the pruning knife with its cruel, curved blade and pulled himself up into the cow's pen. He knelt beside it. Trembling, he sliced into the side of the animal, along the oddly mottled length of hide. It gave easily, opened wide and a burnt smell filled the tent.

The men who had been beating Gabe stopped and watched as Sam pulled open the sides of the bloodless maw. There were no ribs on that side, and curled inside, like an unborn thing, was a naked brownish man with wild black hair and wild dying eyes. The bullets that had punched through the cow had found him, and now blood came snaking from a hole in his throat. Unable to speak, he let out a final breath, a hiss of black mist that went up into Sam's face. Sam gasped, shuddered and toppled from the platform. He lay beside Gabe on the hard dirt floor, dead.

Having been arrested for murder, Gabe sat in a cell for two days, bruised and cold, hugging his cracked ribs. He heard a pair of footsteps approach and looked up to see the chief of police and young Dan Muir. Muir's father had been hired to defend the veterinarian.

"You're all done, here," the officer said, unlocking the cell.

Gabe stared quizzically. "I don't . . . understand . . ."

"The charges against you have been dropped, Doctor Burkett. Go home and try to forget this whole thing. That's what folks around here want to do, forget the whole ungodly mess."

Muir helped Gabe from his bunk, then out to the Model T that, under the circumstances, was a welcome sight.

They drove down the quiet lanes of an autumn afternoon. The air was pleasantly cool and the sun shone bright. Hawks hung free and smaller birds pecked in the harvest fields, unaccosted for the time being.

It did not take Gabriel long to ask the question. "Why did they let me go?"

Dan Muir gave him a strange look. "They said I'm not supposed to say a word to anyone."

Gabe studied him. "But . . .?"

"But I think you ought to know. They performed an autopsy on that man that was in the cow. He wasn't like a man in ways, from what I heard."

"What do you mean?" Gabe asked.

"Well, when they opened his head and looked in his skull, there was this thing in there where his brain should have been. Some kind of an animal, I guess, sort of like a cross between a human fetus and an insect in a larval stage. Its body was all shiny black and segmented, and it had these skinny tendrils running down into his spinal column, and into his major blood vessels."

Gabe stared at the road. "Dear God," he whispered.

"The fellow that did the autopsy wanted to take it to show a professor friend over at Harvard, but the police chief had it burned."

"Good man," Gabe said softly. "Good man."

The smell of baking chicken was emanating from the house. Gabe sat on the porch, watching as the sun mocked the colors of the ridge of trees it was setting behind. His chair creaked as he rocked and he could hear Audrey humming inside.

The days were short now, and October was only hours away. Dreaming off into the deepening heavens, he caught movement from the corner of his eye. A moth had become entangled in a spider web up where one of the porch support beams met the overhanging roof. The moth struggled futilely and the spider poked out from a dark split in the wood and edged out.

Gabe stood, tall man that he was, and reached up. With gentle fingers, he worked delicately to pry the moth from the thin and sticky bands. The brown moth fluttered and went spinning free into the cool air. Gabe stood on the porch and watched as it made its way into the uncertain dusk. He smiled and his smile, as always, was both hopeful and sad.

The Copper Mask

Massachusetts, 1830

After the cider making, after the killing frost, November was close, crouched in the New England hills like a giant old man made of black twigs. The geese knew and the moths, and even the crickets had taken away their summer noise. While bright with sun and seemingly innocuous, it was, in fact, the last day of the tenth month.

Abigail gave it little thought—her mind was on bayberries.

"Good-bye, Mother," the younger Safford said—it being just the two of them since fever had taken her father.

The widow Safford waved from the kitchen door and Abigail was off past the herb beds in her lead-colored dress with a hungry basket swinging; away from the clean white house by the chestnut tree, on the road leading out of town. It was the season of bleak fields and they showed flat amongst the roll of hills; superfluous scarecrows nodding in air cool with secret currents.

Here, under trees and quick shadow, there, squinting in light, Abigail walked, humming, past the edges of the fields, her hair loose and windy, more August than October. The trees that had so recently boasted their plumes of color, were dissolving and the sky, in turn, grew wider by the hour.

The fields reposed—dirt wombs for winter wheat, or scrubby with cut maize, nervous with small birds. Abigail went up hills and down them, stepping between the wagon ruts in the dry October road, humming beneath geese and the crows that called to the straw men with a language only wind would share.

Then came the sweet reek of the dying orchards, the soft browning fruit concealed in triumphant weeds. The buildings of the town were small and toy-like in the distance, the smell of the shops, the clatter of carriages, the voices, hidden by the gray-treed hills. Not to say that there was no color, there were the stubborn gold, defiant red, and frail and bitter yellow awaiting the plucking winds and quiet fingers of frost.

The young woman knew just where to find the sweet bay; off the path, by a meadow near a wood that turned to swamp, hollow with the sound of crows. Abigail waded into the meadow, the dry weeds snatching at her skirt. Birds were in the wood, dark flurrying shapes that tumbled up as pale leaves tumbled down. The bay bushes were hunched together by the bordering trees; their dark leaves had the dull shine of leather. Close to them, Abigail knelt and brushed the hair from her face with the back of her wrist.

The berries that had eluded the birds hung like small black eggs. They were ripe and Abigail gathered them to use in candle making. Humming, she reached into the scented shadows of the bush and stole the fragrant fruit.

West of the October wood, beyond the swamp and the hills heaped like smoke, the light was receding. Shadows in the wood made the trees seem to multiply and a deer, or something large enough to snap twigs, stirred there.

Abigail moved to the next bush, moved to a new tune to hum. Her basket grew heavy, its bounty glinting softly. The smell of the leaves was on her hands and the wind flicked her hair at her eyes.

Sticks snapped in the wood where trees shaped a jail for the light. Abigail leaned to one side to look. A shadow in the shadows—upright—limbs. She stood and stared but the thing had slipped away.

"Hello?"

Again, in the maze of trees, a figure ducked in and out of sight. It was small, dressed darkly. Abigail heard the leaves crisp and rustle beneath its quick steps. The breeze toyed with her hair and she reached to restrain the betraying strands.

"Hello?"

The woman took up her basket and pushed past the bay bushes into the woods, after the boy. It was a boy after all—she had seen his legs, swift in the brittle bracken, the pale hands, his best little Sunday suit. The glimpse had not revealed his head.

"Wait," Abigail called, "Don't be frightened."

The boy thumped away like a rabbit, threading through the bare and near-bare trees, rattling the reluctant colors. Abigail, awkward in her skirt and trying not to dump her berries, fell behind.

"Wait, won't you?"

Every step rasped where the maples had bled and squat pines like green shadows obstructed the peripheral child. Sometimes Abigail could see his arms waving, his hands plucking leaves as he went. Other times it was his back and once, where bone-colored birches stood thin in the gloom, she spied his whole body and, in that compromised afternoon light, there was no head.

The sky was widening beyond the trees, a wistful blue. The small dark shape of the boy burst out of the wood, into the air, and Abigail lost sight of him. Breathing hard, she slowed, stepped over roots and crippled boughs. Good Massachusetts hills rose beyond a field and the wood fell behind.

Pumpkins hugged the ground in the dimming light, like orange turtles half-tucked under wide leaves. Abigail did not see the boy—perhaps he was lying among the crops, close to the cool earth. She stepped carefully through the fragile vines, peering down.

"Hello?"

Her voice went out across the field, to the hulking ghost hills, gray like ash, red where maples still burned.

There was no sign of the boy. Abigail moved on, deeper into the pumpkin patch, her two feet crunching as she stepped around the many-sized globes. Near the middle of the field, she found a number of dead crows, neatly folded about themselves, there in the withering leaves. They were dark against the yellowed grass, shimmering softly, as if damp in faltering light. Abigail was about to stoop for a closer look, but a sharp glint of light caught her eye. Like a crow herself, Abigail was drawn to the spark and, upon inspection, saw something metal tucked close to the pumpkins and crows.

She bent and lifted the copper mask. How it gleamed! A simple, elegant face comprised of metal leaves, cool and light in the hand. It stared back impassively, the eyes cut out. How could she not put it on?

Forgetting all about the boy, Abigail placed the mask over her face and it held there as if pushed by wind. She shot up and her hair flung out like a scream. She saw the world through the October mask—the falling light, the decaying fields, the crows, the round hills where November perched in its cold black bones.

Acorns, rose hips, gourds, and winter squash. Ash, sycamore, oak, and silver maple. The road led through the last day of the tenth month. The light was weary and, like the mask, coppery as it knelt upon the fields. Abigail walked as if sleeping, her basket of berries swaying gently.

She passed two men harvesting turnips, their cart heaped and smelling of earth. Gazing through the mask, Abigail saw the first, pale as a swan, his eyes dead in deep smudges. The other, oblivious, about his task, appeared charred where his flesh showed. A small clay pipe was clenched in his teeth, his lips burnt away.

It was the same in town, where Abigail walked in her copper guise. Death, beneath the mask of flesh, was hers in all its future faces. Unconcealed, the townsfolk showed her these faces—this one shriveled in age, that one gashed in mishap, others bloated, blue, pocked, wasted with disease.

It was the same with the houses, lonely and dim in the dusk-draped town. The sun was lost, down through the trees, like a big brass kettle, glinting its last. The twilight breeze mocked the ocean in the leaves. The moon was on the sky like breath on glass.

One house after the other showed Abigail its sorry face. Up from the weeds, a peaked behemoth of moldering gingerbread stood, its paint in the moonlight like the scales of crumbling fish. Wind sounded in the vacant stairwells, behind the hollow windows with nothing in their darkness but strange eyes like dislocated stars.

Down the street, house after house. Dolls with crabapple eyes, in a house filled with dark water, hovered like slow pale fish in the windows. The sinuous foliage of a willow waved from the chimney like tentacles of smoke.

Her own house crumbling gray beneath the chestnut, Abigail kicked her way up the leafy path to the door. Inside and quiet as could be, she peered into the kitchen. She was thankful that her mother's back was to her, afraid to see what was on the other side of the crone-colored hair. Her mother was singing quietly, the words strained and muffled as if fumbling through a broken mouth.

Up the drafty stairs, past walls dripping spiders, Abigail sought her bedchamber. The frosty light of the moon was on the window. A mirror hung above her chest of clothes and she stood in front of it, her full skirt rustling as if there were only leaves beneath. The copper mask was dim in the glass and it was likely the improbable light that made Abigail imagine the mouth of the mask opening, a beak and maybe the dark of a bird's head poking briefly from between her teeth.

The mask that had seemed so light, now ached against her features and Abigail lay on her dusty bed beneath the great copper weight.

November seemed gray and brown, its light weak as if shone through milk. Widow Safford stirred over breakfast, the scents warm in the clean, tidy kitchen. Ferns of frost were on the window glass, a kettle on the stove.

"Abigail," her mother called.

Her daughter must not have felt well—hadn't she gone up to her sleep early the night before?

"Abigail, breakfast . . ."

Her calls went up the stairs without reply. Widow Safford sighed and went up herself. She rapped softly at the door and called through the wood.

"Abigail?"

When she opened the door, Abigail's mother saw the room was dark but for chill November light falling on the bed, where damp dead crows made the shape of a body, its face a copper mask.

The Franklin Stove

North-Central Massachusetts

Poor Aunt Hattie, she can never get warm. Here it is only December and already she pines for June. But is it really any wonder, in a cavernous old house like this, with more shadows than drapes and more drafts than rugs?

Perhaps if she had some more meat on her bones things might be different. You would think she would be round and plush, the way she indulges her appetite for baked goods, but this is not the case. In summertime her dresses hang off her frame as if laundry on a line, and even in winter her fortifying layers droop.

Aunt Hattie is stingy with firewood. Even a girl my age can tell that is part of her problem. There is a brooding black Franklin stove in the parlor, yet she only feeds it a quarter-log at a time. Not until one stick is all but burnt out does she add another, propping it against the pitiful remnants of its predecessor. Whether the added piece lights or not is largely a thing of chance.

The frugality of this method often leads to a string of under-the-breath curses as Auntie scrabbles together kindling to re-light the stove. During my visits I occasionally sneak extra wood into the firebox (at the risk of a scolding).

I have mentioned that it is December. Snow has come to the region and it makes the house look gray. It's a tall house, a staggered thing of peaks and angles and windows of varied size. Each generation of occupants has built onto it so that now it is difficult to visualize the original structure. Even Uncle Abner (rest his soul) tried his hand. Poor fellow never did earn any blue ribbons for carpentry, as evidenced by his addition. The clapboards swell as if over a secret too big to contain, and it appears to lean against other parts of the house, seems to rely on them to keep it standing.

Today the house looks uncomfortable, towering in the cold, staring out over the lumps that denote a smothered garden. Beyond it the wide white yard is striped blue with the shadows of trees.

I am making a snowman. Aunt Hattie watches from the kitchen window, shrouded in a throw. She waves and I wave back, my mitten damp and clumpy.

Sunlight glares on the panes and for a brief moment I imagine a tall, severe woman in mourning black glaring out over my aunt's shoulder.

What my snowman lacks in symmetry he makes up for in charm. His walnut eyes beam along a carrot nose and the sprigs of fir I've used for hair sprout jauntily from his crown.

In the window Aunt Hattie applauds silently and smiles at my crooked masterpiece. The veiled woman behind her is gone. Strange. There seems to be a scattering of snow on my aunt's shoulders.

There is such a clattering of pans from the kitchen that I half expect to find suits of armor wrestling on the floor when I enter. Auntie is on her knees with her head stuck in a low cupboard; she is looking for her favorite baking dish.

"I thought," she says between clangs, "we'd make an apple pandowdy in honor of your visit."

"Pandowdy!" I exclaim. She knows it's my favorite.

"Oh, Dear, would you please close the door? There's such a draft!"

I push the door shut with my rump, then put down my armload of firewood. Auntie rises triumphant, clutching her dish to her chest like a breastplate.

We divide the preparatory tasks; I remove the crusts from bread slices, then tear them into fingers to dip in melted butter. Aunt Hattie peels, cores, and slices the apples.

Once all has been assembled, and fruit and cinnamon scent the room, we sprinkle dark brown sugar across the top layer.

How curious. Afternoon light catches on a few white flecks that flutter down before the lid is placed over the dish. I turn and look up, and see a dusting of white powder on Aunt Hattie's shoulders.

The old woman shudders. "Ohhh, my bones feel like icicles."

I glimpse the hem of a black skirt whisking from the room.

Aunt Hattie judiciously chooses a piece of wood and places it in the Franklin. The doors squeal, clang shut, and the stove sits there ticking like a big black clock.

Waiting for the pandowdy to bake, I am patience on a stool while my aunt plays with my hair. She tries a number of styles, each time taking a step back and cocking her head as she studies her handiwork. She offers a hand mirror so that I can admire myself. I notice that cinnamon from the kitchen work has added to my freckles and I rub my cheek with a wrist.

"You look lovely," Auntie says, delighted, "just like your Aunt Clara when she was your age."

It is a rare occasion when my aunt mentions her deceased sister.

Clara died when I was just a baby. It was a tragic thing, and my father might never have told me the details were it not for an overindulgence of Christmas cheer (and even then I was sworn never to repeat them).

The elderly spinster Clara had moved in with Aunt Hattie shortly after Uncle Abner passed on. One bitter night in December the sisters sat by the Franklin reading, as was their nightly ritual. Hattie dozed off in her rocker and when she awoke her sister was gone from the chair opposite. Assuming that Clara had gone up to bed, Hattie locked the doors and retired to her own chamber.

Hattie is a sound sleeper. Unaware that her sister had trudged out to fetch wood for the fire, she slumbered peacefully through the desperate, then slowing thumps at the door.

Clara, alone in her crisis, was either too weak or disoriented to smash a window, it seems. Hattie found the body in the morning, as brittle as a frozen sparrow.

The day dims now, the sun faltering behind dark firs, leaving smears of muffled peach. The house is warmer for the smell of pandowdy, but the shadows increase.

Auntie hands me the mirror so that I can witness her latest creation. My hair is piled like a bee skep.

"Oh, very fancy!" I say, giggling.

I hold the mirror; the reflection shows a charcoal figure in the window behind me. She is stiff against the quieting sky, haggard behind a veil that shifts like smoke. A chill goes up my neck and I drop the mirror. It smashes as if it were ice.

The apple pandowdy is done at last and it is glorious. We enjoy it with fresh whipped cream, close by the Franklin (a banker's safe full of precious heat).

The stove is hot, the food is hot and the tea is hot, but still Aunt Hattie shivers.

"I'm so cold," she moans.

The sky has darkened above the chalk world and the jumbled gray house in which we sit. We have drained our tea and scraped every bit of pandowdy from our plates. I take these to the kitchen and wash them, content and humming.

Some little time passes and an unpleasant odor comes to me on the air. I hear a dull repetition of thumps.

"Auntie?"

Drying my hands, I walk back to the parlor. The room is full of terrible black smoke. At first I can scarcely make out the figure of my aunt, her head stuffed into the roaring red mouth of the Franklin stove, her body slumped behind.

The thumping of her feet slows and stops as frosty handprints on her upper back melt into her shawl.

I shriek and run from the room, racing through the kitchen and out the side door. I trip over some large folded thing that lies across the walkway.

Righting myself, I catch a glimpse of a rising darkness, its icy eyes glaring behind a veil.

I scream all the way home.

Widow's Pond

Back in past times there was a pond by a pathway. Villagers traveled the path heedlessly in their daily affairs, but at night, all who knew better took other routes; for it was told, and much believed, that a night traveler would encounter at the pond a woman dressed in the garb of mourning.

She would sit, it was said, on a log, gazing at the ominous pond waters and awaiting the return of her lost love.

One misty night, in olden days, a man came riding along. He was a traveling craftsman looking for a village in which to sell his skills, perhaps even settle. He came to the spot where the woods gave way to a watery expanse; a cool and fetid disk ringed with particularly gnarled vegetation. At first he did not see the woman, for it was dark and the moon was a mere pale reflection on the calm pool's murk.

The woman's age was hard to place, such were the shadows about her veiled face. But her hands, wringing a cloth, were very light and they beckoned him nearer to the log on which she sat.

"Oh lonely traveler, come sit by my side.

And watch with me, sir, as the water bugs glide."

"I've no time, my dear woman," the traveler said.
"A village I need, some food and a bed."

The woman stood slowly, a hand outstretched. She stepped toward the rider, her voice flowing softly, "Oh, lonely traveler, come sit by my pond,
Its dark oily waters a door to beyond.
Obsidian treasures await you below.
Come walk with me, sir, in depths of black snow."

The widow stood by the man's tall horse. She lay her pearly fingers on his thigh. The man let out a cry and lurched back from his mount, into the sullen pool.
"Dark sweet death," the widow cried.
"Drink it in deep, you fool!"
He bobbed up once, but he looked like bones,
and was sucked down in a blink where the cold depth moans.

Wrought-Iron Skeleton

Massachusetts, 1877

Mrs. Trowbridge painted the bones of animal skeletons once the flesh was boiled away. Then, in autumn, when the leaves got their color, she hung them in the surrounding woods, as if the maples, birches, and sumacs weren't enough. Never one for wire, she fastened the bones together with string or yarn where necessary, but over time those materials weathered and the bright, dangling skeletons transformed. Some of their parts might be missing, or sections might appear unnaturally elongated due to the stretching of damp yarn. In these cases, the bones became the remains of creatures not fumbled upon by evolution, or perhaps the echo of things that strolled the globe before man took up the quill to record them.

I have forever possessed an interest in antiquated objects and while Mrs. Trowbridge was something of a relic in her own right, it was not *her* bones that I sought that morning when I volunteered to help those who had gathered to seek for her earthly shell. In all honesty, I was looking for *things*. Considering her age (ninety-something, if memory serves), I thought I might come upon some hoary treasures in the sooty heap that had been her old saltbox.

The smoke seemed to have settled in the trees, lending a touch of sepia to the autumnal mist common to October mornings. Small skeletons rattled in the low branches when we brushed past them and things that I hoped were only birch twigs snapped under foot.

I have never been accused of philanthropy, which is not to say that I'm as unscrupulous as those "salvagers" who would lure a ship to rocky reefs in order to reap a soggy reward. Still, I was not one to slight opportunity. Once or twice (all right, seven times) I had set upon nocturnal forays into the homes of antediluvian locals who, busy making amends with their Creator, seemed not to mind my rummaging about their dark rooms for collectibles.

I kept an ear open for word of funerals, scheduling my adventures accordingly. Sometimes it was a race against the departed's ravenous offspring, but most of the time the houses sat empty and I was at my leisure to go about my hunting.

One time, however, I misheard a bit of dialogue and consequently stole into a place where an old woman was apparently *near* death and not actually in its possession. The word of Spinster Spooner's funeral—in the fragment of conversation that I had perceived—turned out to be a prediction, not an arrangement.

There I was in the middle of the night, in a great rambling tomb of a house, when suddenly the ghastly figure of the hag shot up in her bed. I started of course, but calling swiftly upon my resourceful nature, I noted that she had a carving of that poor thorn-crowned fellow hanging over her bed. I promptly and (very earnestly) mentioned to her that I was Saint so and so, come to see her off. Well, with that she gave me a blissful little smile then settled back and went about her death rattle. I came away with a few handsome items that night—but I've digressed!

At any rate, that clammy morning I had joined the rest trudging through damp leaves to the burned wreckage of the Trowbridge house. I received my share of suspicious glances from the boys of the fire brigade because, as mentioned, I was not known for my generosity and thus my motives were likely to be questioned. At least they had the restraint not to accuse me outright of anything unsavory.

The house had been a fine specimen of 18th-century construction, but now it was one of God's smashed toys, a few upright fragments of rooms seemingly resting atop a baroque nest of blackened timber. A shame, really, for the house *and* the occupant. The fire seemed to have started on an upper level, according to witnesses of the previous night. An attempt had been made to rescue the widow, and one fellow swore he saw a figure stumbling about behind the flames, but the blaze drove them out from the first floor. The body was not recovered, thus our morning stroll in the burnt-smelling mist.

Looking at the ruin, I harbored little hope of finding anything worth taking, and even if there were treasures, they would need to be of concealable size. I hoped I would not be the one to actually discover the scorched corpus and, as it turns out, I was not.

"Dear heavens!" a Mr. Needham—one of the more ethical volunteers—exclaimed.

He stepped back from the blackened mess where he had been prodding with his stick.

"I expected her to be burnt," he said, "but there's not a trace of flesh upon her."

While moments before I had dreaded the thought of such a discovery, I suddenly found myself as morbidly inclined as any young fellow and hastened to view the horror.

Tangled among the dark wreckage, partly obscured by ash and mud and morning shadows, lay an adult-sized assemblage of blackened bones, which, despite the gray day and the debris, had something of a gleam to it. I puzzled and tapped the ribs with my cane; the sound was distinctly metallic.

"I don't believe that's *her*," I noted.

The others gathered and the undertaker, Bellows, put his hands on the thing, determining that it certainly was not what was left of Mrs. Trowbridge. He tapped his knuckles on the forehead of the grinning skull.

"Wrought iron," he noted.

We all turned to look at Simon Perry, the blacksmith, as if he might have an explanation.

"Don't look to me," he said.

"Curious." I was intrigued.

"Whatever *is* it?" Needham, the volunteer asked.

Even though the "bones" were formed of metal and not Adam's rib, it seemed as if the undertaker was burdened with the task of authority. The blacksmith stood stupefied alongside the rest of us.

"Well, it appears to be a replica of sorts. She always did like bones."

"Queer old woman," Simon Perry muttered.

I noticed something just then. "Look there, how she must have positioned that bucket in its hands, as if it were fetching water."

There was still a trace of ash-colored liquid in the vessel.

Before long Mrs. Trowbridge was uncovered. While she was not cooked down to the bone, she was quite charred, and the smell was something I'd rather forget. She was gently lifted from the devastation and wrapped in a sheet before being slid onto the back of a wagon.

The party of volunteers and brigade men slowly broke up. I went to have another look at the metal skeleton lying half-buried under boards and falling leaves. It was darker than the seared wood, the hollow eyes so vacant. It chilled me to think that we living beings harbor anything like that ghastly visage beneath our soft, pretty flesh. Still, there was a beauty to it, conjoined with my horror.

As it turns out I was the last to leave. I had found no trinkets worth pocketing, nor, for whatever reason, did I seem to care. I headed off along the path away from the house, into the woods where brick-colored bird bones floated under dissipating maples and the smeary blue skeleton of a raccoon swayed, clattering in the breeze that came up to shoo off the mist.

I had come into possession of a large center-hall house dating from 1774, complete with wide "King's timber" pine floors and great twin chimneys. The fireplaces were set flush in the baronial paneled walls and the exterior corners boasted wooden quoins. It was a wonder of symmetry and grace.

It was at this house, one fine October evening, that I entertained a small party of close friends. Idle chatter was an art that I had long mastered, as good a diversion as drink or flirtation, though I may have liked it best when the three were combined. That night I was in top form.

A chill warranted the crackling pile of birch and the brandy that followed dinner offered heat of its own. My dear friend Richard had brought along his latest fiancé, the giggly Madeline. She burst into unscrupulous laughter at one of my more imprudent jokes and dashed theatrically out of the parlor, her skirt—the size of a circus tent—hissing past the hearth.

A sudden scream shrilled and a very pale version of Madeline came rushing out of my adjacent study, a hand to her considerable bosom.

"Maddy?" I said innocently.

"What *is* that thing?" she demanded.

I chuckled; all eyes had turned from Madeline's bosom to me.

"The skeleton? Yes, a marvel, isn't it?"

The others rose from their seats and went to investigate. There, standing like a starved, blackened suit of armor in a corner of my study, was the wrought-iron mystery I had salvaged from the Trowbridge ruins.

"And how much did you pay for that?" Richard asked. Richard's nerves were wrought iron, so he was not as appalled as the others.

"I found it. Very life like—or should I say *death-like*, isn't it?"

Madeline peeked back in over Richard's shoulder and asked in an accusatory tone, "Why would you want a thing like that?"

"It's unique, for one. It's also a marvel of craftsmanship. My physician tells me that it is correct in every detail."

Richard was warming to the thing. "It is an interesting piece, I suppose, but a bit on the morbid side."

"Perhaps that's the appeal." I gave them a devilish smile. All collectors are guilty of a measure of madness, and my friends knew this and loved me for it. "More brandy!"

Imagine my horror when I woke the next morning to find my front door lying in the frost and my wrought iron skeleton gone from the house.

Not even Richard would have taken a joke so far. It was a malicious act, really, and if it was meant to be humorous, it entirely missed its mark. I promptly dismissed my few disgruntled servants (despite their proclamations of innocence) and set out to find the heavy black anomaly.

It was obviously the work of more than one culprit, for no single man—even a powerful man—could have moved that thing the mile and a half distance I traversed to find it. Apparently they had dragged the skeleton, for there was a broken trail leading the way, the frosty leaves displaced, the damp grass gouged by the hard black foot bones.

"Oh, clever," I said, leaning on my stick, having followed the trail to the cheerless black heap that had been Mrs. Trowbridge's house. Reddish leaves sprinkled down and skittered over the tragic clutter.

It was the most elaborate prank I had ever witnessed, and if it had been someone other than myself on the receiving end, I'd have admired the effort.

They had taken the skeleton and positioned it face down amongst the charred boards, going so far as to dig a hole to accommodate the bulk of the iron torso, suggesting that the thing had been burrowing.

I hired some men to return the sculpture to my home and hired others to return my door to its hinges and add a number of secure locks. I was furious, the more so for my confusion. Perhaps, I speculated, it was the wretched town folk behind the violation—they all harbored a certain bitterness toward me, after all. It was envy no doubt, because of my position, because my fortune came from an inheritance rather than my sweat. To Hell with them all, I thought.

A long night of brooding and brandy followed as I prowled the old house with my pistol in hand, my curses hissing off into unlit corners.

I sat and stared at the impassive face of the skeleton, its surface both smooth and ridged, and I wondered with a quiet sense of awe about the construction of such an armature (both the fine piece of jointed metal work and the bone original it was modeled after). Whether one dubbed it God or evolution, *some* form of genius had been at work.

Still, even more impressive than that, more a mystery than bone and muscle and tendons and organs, was the force of life and the sentience that occupied and animated the corporeal human vehicle.

Those were my thoughts before I dozed at the desk, before the aroma of coffee seeped into my dream and summoned my consciousness into the cool bronze of October's morning light. There were birds in the garden, but not the hungry, territorial birds of spring—there was a purposeful urgency now in their cries as they plotted their travels south.

The coffee was stronger than I like and some had spilled on the desk near to where my own sleeping skull had weighed. It took me a moment, and a sip of the brew, to remember that I had dismissed all the servants, and I had no recollection of preparing the stuff. I held the cup away and eyed it quizzically, but then my eyes fell upon the corner where the skeleton should have stood.

The wrought-iron skeleton gleamed. It stood outside in the light and spitting leaves, solemn and black, rigid on the granite stoop. The head turned to face me, the teeth clenched as it regarded me with its inscrutable scooped-out stare.

I must have mirrored its rigidity just then, as a shock of horror shot through every limb; but a moment later I was like a rag fluttering back into the hallway. I slammed the door shut and fumbled the locks, a whole herd of hearts in my chest.

It was another trick, of course, a puppet, or something like those clever mechanized dolls that jerk their heads and wag their arms in the windows of Boston toyshops.

I heard the thump of a footfall and rushed to the parlor, where I pulled aside the drapes and peered out. The skeleton took an awkward step, then another. I gasped. It was *walking*.

Despite the lumbering aspect of its motions, the skeleton conveyed something that I could only term as determination as it started out along the road, rasping through the fallen leaves.

I rushed to throw a coat over my sleeping gown and hastened into my boots, a fever of exclamations firing from my lips. As a last minute thought, I grabbed my pistol from the study and headed out to follow the skeleton.

It had not progressed far when I caught up with it. I hung back, naturally, shivering, trying not to make noise, despite the broken pavement of leaves. How stark it looked against a background of autumn colors as it jerked along, the head turning ever so slightly from side to side as if looking for something.

We ended up at the sad disarray of the Trowbridge house. The iron figure stood with its hands on its cold hammered hips, surveying the scene.

I suppose I could go on for pages about my feelings on that cold golden morning, but I'll spare you the bulk of it and only say that a thousand thoughts were in my brain. There was awe and terror, fascination and dread—all these things colliding, and then, in a predominant flush . . . sadness.

The thing of iron bones waded into the wreckage and began sifting through the sooty boards. Its body creaked and the boards clattered, tossed aside. It stooped and stared and went on in this relentless manner for some time before standing and turning to face me. While incapable of expression, there was a questioning quality to the action.

What does one say to a metal skeleton?

"Mrs. Trowbridge...is that . . . *you?*"

The neck squealed as the head shook back and forth.

It seemed the obvious explanation at the time that this strange sculpture was somehow a vessel for the disembodied spirit of the old woman who had died in the blaze.

"No," I muttered, "not Mrs. Trowbridge. Would you then be the spirit of Mrs. Trowbridge's deceased husband?"

No again.

"Then who are you?"

Again the head wagged.

"Don't you know?"

I shuddered as the thing took a step toward me. Brittle bits of blackened wood snapped beneath its weight and leaves hissed and kicked up as it walked within feet of me. Staring, and in response to my inquiry, it shrugged, its metal joints squeaking.

I suppose none us truly knows what elusive spark holds up our frail figures, be it a spirit or soul, or some other force as yet unimagined by our limited minds. All we even know of our selves are our personalities. This creature, as it turns out, would prove similar in that aspect—I would never learn who or what occupied that black assemblage of parts, but a form of madness had overtaken me, for I found myself urging the thing to follow me back to the house.

It stood hovering in the parlor until I told it to sit. The chair did not care for the idea, groaning beneath the weight of my guest. Dusk softened the windows and a chill came on as I knelt at the hearth and started a fire. The skeleton watched, leaning forward, seemingly in great interest.

I could only imagine what my friends would have thought had they come around that evening. There I sat, talking to so many pounds of upright black iron as if it were alive.

Sadly, there was no way for the thing to properly communicate, although I did test it some.

"Do you know where your head is?"

A thin black arm rose and the hand pointed to its skull.

"Where are your feet?"

It pointed again.

"Did you bring me coffee this morning?"

It nodded. I was thrilled, fascinated.

"So, you prepared the coffee by yourself?"

The skeleton nodded.

I thought for a moment and hesitantly asked, "Should I fear you?"

It shook its head; no.

I smiled. "Well, then, seeing as we seem to be on friendly terms, I'll just have to teach you how to write so that our interchanges won't be so one sided. Would you like to learn to write?"

The skeleton nodded enthusiastically, the neck squealing.

In the morning there was coffee. It seems the skeleton had managed the stairs, for the brew was on the table by my bed when I awoke.

Once again the skeleton had gone out into the morning, back to the ruin. I found it rummaging about in the boards, a strangely graceful creature in that it was thin and slow. I wish I knew what it was looking for, but I'd wondered if perhaps it missed its old friend.

"Good morning," I said.

It looked up and nodded then turned back to its task.

"Thank you for the coffee."

I received a small bow, but then it was back to its business.

After thinking a moment I inquired, "Excuse me . . . are you looking for Mrs. Trowbridge?"

The skeleton shot up and I started, stepping back. The thing nodded eagerly.

"Mrs. Trowbridge is dead," I said.

It stared at me—there was no perceivable reaction.

"Do you understand *dead*?"

The skeleton shook its head.

I sighed. "Come with me back to the house. It's time for your lessons."

My companion followed me along the road, past the lake—the trees had made a great ring of color around it and the sun was trying to penetrate the dark waters.

Considering the fact that I was never inclined toward rearing children, I exhibited a great deal of patience when it came to the schooling of my pupil. The skeleton caught on quickly—in no time it was writing the alphabet, although it had an awkward time holding the quill initially.

I taught the student my name and asked it if it, too, had a title, if the old woman had called it something. It nodded and wrote "J".

The lessons became a daily routine, as with the visits to the Trowbridge wreckage where the skeleton continued to scrounge.

Within weeks the skeleton was writing words and added some letters to its name.

"John. She called you John?"

The skeleton nodded.

"Well then," I said, "how nice to meet you, John." I held out my hand and my friend took it in its icy black fingers and shook it gently.

We found a dead half-grown fox by the road the next morning. It was peaceful-looking and bore no sign of injury. John knelt by it, creaking, and prodded the silvery mass.

"It's dead, John, the poor little creature. *Dead.*"

Leaves made soft clicks as they fell in the near wood.

"John, it's like the bones that Mrs. Trowbridge hung in the trees—whatever property was within to make them alive has ceased, or perhaps moved on."

John looked at me with his hollow eyes and then pointed off toward his old home.

"Yes," I said, "dead, like Mrs. Trowbridge."

The skeleton returned its gaze to the fox.

"I'll show you what we do with the dead, John. Come, we'll bring it back to the house and give it a burial."

Much like a child who imitates the actions of a parent, John had taken to reproducing mine. He took a turn digging the hole and helped pad the earth down over the small grave.

"Some people pray about this time," I explained, "but I think that concept might be a bit complicated at this point."

While John could offer little to nothing in regards to his origin and history, he was getting to the point where he could formulate crude sentences. One evening, when the month was drawing to its end and the trees were mostly bare against the wide moon-tinted sky, we sat about my desk in the study. His face gleamed strangely in the candlelight.

He wrote: SHE WAS COLD. I MADE FIRE. BAD BAD BURN.

I began to understand. I nodded. "Mrs. Trowbridge was cold, so you tried to make a fire to get her warm, but the house went up . . . "

Now John nodded. I remembered back when we found him in the rubble, holding the bucket, and how there was a trace of water left in it.

"You tried to put out the fire?"

A nod. Then he wrote: SORRY SORRY SORRY.

I gathered myself. "Well, John, you meant well and you did the right thing. You tried. You did the good thing, John, you tried to save her."

WHERE MRS? John wrote.

I put a hand on his cold shoulder. "She's buried, in the ground, like the fox. You remember the fox?"

He nodded and then he pushed his chair back and seemed to gaze off into the fireplace where the flames were licking up through the maple logs and the smoke made ghosts.

A touch of snow had fallen in the night—no more than a dusting, but it gave the world an ethereal quality as it softened the road and lightened the shadows under the leafless trees.

There was coffee waiting when I awoke and a piece of paper by that. I sat in my bed, tasted the coffee and took up the note. It was crudely written; a single sentiment emerging from the sepia of coffee stains: GOOD BYE.

I dressed in a rush and started for the Trowbridge house. John's steps were in the snow — odd patterns left by the metal bones. I followed the tracks, but they did not lead to the Trowbridge ruins; they led to the great black circle of the lake. The tracks led *into* the lake.

I caught my breath and stood there looking out at the water, its dark stillness, the empty trees ringed gray around it. I muttered a name—a metal skeleton's name, of all things, and I had to laugh at that. I gave a small laugh so that I would not cry.

I've kept the lessons that John wrote and the final coffee-stained message. I take them from my desk and ponder them on occasion. Once in a while, and mostly in October, I walk out to the lonely boards that were the Trowbridge house. Weeds have claimed the place—resilient, unthinking entities that they are.

Generally, I stop at the edge of the lake on my way back to the house. It's a quiet spot and the colored leaves spin down to the water and settle on the surface. I imagine John somewhere out in that deep water, lying at the bottom, rusting to the color of autumn leaves.

Sharp Medicine

Many years ago, before there were motorcars and electrical machines, there was a large farm in a small New England town. For the sake of the story let's imagine that this is the very site of the happenings I'm about to relate . . .

Nathan Bell, his wife and two children lived at the far edge of a healthy tract of land. Their home was a fine and sturdy thing, bordered on two sides by deep woods. The front faced the distant buildings of the village proper, and of course, there was the swamp . . . a dank and dimly lit expanse stretching along the western edge of the Bell property.

Nathan and his wife Emma gave strict orders to their children not to wander into the swamp.

"Who knows what manner of dangerous wild beasts might dwell in there?" Mr. Bell asked in his deep, stern voice.

The children, Betsy, who was ten, and James, whose age was twelve, listened with wide eyes. They knew better than to cross their father. Besides, the swamp *was* a fearful place—even on the brightest of days it seemed unnaturally shaded, and the air was sickly-thick with decaying leaves and stagnant water.

Life for the Bells was generally good. There was always hard work to be done and the finicky New England weather was at times challenging, but their farm was prosperous. That spring when the troubles started, the sheep had been sheared and the planting was done. Nathan believed it would be their best year yet.

Dusk was blurring the eastern sky when young Betsy spied a strange figure coming out of the swamp. Alone, but for a hug-worn doll, the girl ducked down so that the stranger would not notice her. He was a spindly old thing with long, white, unkempt hair. He had a muddy shovel resting across one shoulder as he headed across one of the Bell's newly sown fields. The curious girl followed him from behind.

The figure slowed as he got close to the farmhouse and barn. He seemed to be staggering, weakening as he went. Betsy could have sworn she heard a low moaning sound coming from the man, but it may have been the sudden chill of wind blowing in from the west, carrying with it the musty smell of the swamp. She noticed that the man was carrying a cloth sack in one hand. It made a clattering sound as it swayed. As the old fellow slowed, the distance between him and the girl shrank until at last he spun around, startling her.

"Girl!" the old man said, his eyes staring wide from a pale bony face. "I am not well!"

Betsy Bell was too frightened to respond. She stood gawking up at the trembling, wheezing image of the stranger as the contents of the cloth bag rattled. The man bent down and stuffed the sack into the girl's hand. He mumbled something that she could not make out, and then collapsed.

The girl ran the rest of the way to the house. She called to her parents, who followed her out into the fields.

When they reached the point where the girl had claimed they would find the fallen stranger, Nathan frowned and gave Betsy a bewildered look.

"He was there, Papa, I swear—he fell right there!"

The old man was gone.

Mrs. Bell pointed at the freshly turned, newly seeded soil and said, "Look, Nathan, there are marks . . ."

It was as if something had been dragged. They followed the lines to the edge of the western field, a good many yards from where the poor old fellow had dropped. He was lying on his back, his head turned, eyes looking off into the swamp like two wide coins. He was dead.

They never did learn much about the man . . . not even his name. Talk of the mystery spread though the town. Some claimed he matched the description of a man who was thrown out of a tavern in Southborough for acting in a disorderly manner. The man, it was told, had boasted drunkenly about all the graves he had robbed and all the ancient artifacts he had stolen from the earth. He claimed that he had found the remains of an old settlement dating back before the Indians, but would not disclose the location for fear that others might rob him of the treasures there. When several locals mocked him, he flew into a violent rage and, in turn, found himself tossed out on his skinny rump.

Well, the old fellow was buried in the potter's field, and within a few weeks he was forgotten. Nathan Bell took the cloth bag and tossed it into the cellar, where it and the flaked-stone arrowheads it contained were also put out of mind.

Several months passed. Summer came and the crops grew tall. The madness struck the sheep first. They became skittish, then began making strange noises in the middle of the night. Emma Bell woke one evening and thought she heard garbled voices coming from the barn.

When her husband went out to investigate, he also heard them, but he could make no sense of the words being spoken, if they were indeed words. When he flung the barn door open the sheep fell silent.

The Bells became more concerned when the normally passive sheep became rowdy. Several even tried to trample the children. The town reverend was summoned. He suggested they try "sharp medicine"—slitting the throats of the afflicted animals to release the evil that had polluted them. Nathan Bell picked the most demented creatures from the flock and spilled their blood. For a while, things seemed to return to normal.

Summer dwindled, the long days of heat and haze yielding to the chill encroachment of autumn. The days were crammed with work as the harvest kept the Bell family busy. The bracken that spanned the dark length of swamp blazed gold and the leaves in the nearby woods began to crisp and color. Ironically, the beauty of the season ushered in the decay of the year.

One night Nathan woke to find his wife was missing. He searched the house, but did not find her. Then he heard the sound of hammering echoing out in the fields. He took a lantern and followed the sound beyond the apple trees and pumpkin patch. He found his wife, her nightgown splotched with dirt, her hair stringy with sweat. She was banging boards together. Mrs. Bell had made a box of impressive size, big enough to hold a good-sized pony, or several humans. She had also dug a hole large enough to hold the box.

"Wife!" the man exclaimed, "what in God's name are you doing?"

"I am doing *nothing* in God's name!" she hissed, walking toward him with the hammer.

When Nathan awoke his head was hot with pain and he was in

cramped wooden darkness. He listened as shovel-full after shovel-full of dirt thumped dully on the roof of the box.

"He said something about going into the swamp to trap snapping turtles," Emma Bell lied to the villagers who inquired about her husband's sudden disappearance. The poor children were shattered by the loss of their father. Search teams tried in vain to find the man in the dim and fetid swamp west of the farm. Neighbors offered to help the woman with the harvesting of crops, but she angrily declined their kindness and the produce rotted in the fields.

Now, no one knows exactly just where Nathan Bell was buried alive, but they claim it was under this very field over which we now breathe. It was also here, on a cold drizzle-gray night, that young Betsy ventured after hearing the pathetic banging of the trapped man. She could hear his voice rising vague and strained though the dirt and wood.

"Papa? Is that you, Papa?" Betsy called.

The next sound the girl heard was not a muffled voice, but the familiar bony clatter of flint arrowheads in a cloth sack. She turned to see a figure in a damp white gown moving slowly across the field.

"Betsy . . . ," her mother called. "Betsy . . . "

A strange and dreadful chill ran through the girl's blood. Her mother came closer, until Betsy could make out her features—the eyes wild, like some rabid animal's, the mouth drawn in a hideous sneering smile. The woman's breath was like the stagnant waters of the bordering swamp.

"Come to mother, my dear girl," the woman beckoned, "I must kill you."

Betsy broke into a run. Tears and drizzle blurred her vision as she rambled fright-maddened through the fields. She ducked into a twitching sea of raspy cornstalks, hearing the clatter of stone arrowheads bouncing against each other; and there were other sounds as well. She heard those strange garbled voices that had come from the sheep barn. Looking back, she saw her mother running barefoot through the damp haze, followed by a number of hobbling semi-decomposed sheep, their heads swaying and limp, barely attached—the throats cut wide by sharp medicine.

Betsy crashed through the cornstalks, crying, her heart drumming. She had to reach help, she had to escape from that unearthly hunts-pack behind her! She did not notice the scarecrow until she collided with it.

Her shrieks echoed through the night. The scarecrow was the body of her brother James, roped to stakes, his head slack to one side. When the girl thudded against the corpse, the mouth fell open and a number of slate arrowheads came spilling out.

Do you see that tree there? That's where the village folk found the girl Betsy, swinging from a rope; so they say. But this is a very old tale, and time has a way of stretching the past into strange and remarkable shapes. You're welcome to believe this story if you wish. Who am I to say what's true or not?

People about these parts claim this place is haunted, still. One old woman claims it rained arrowheads one spring night, that these old fields were scattered with them. She says that the townsfolk gathered them into wheelbarrows and dumped them in the swamp. Others claim to have seen the bony figure of that strange old man hobbling across the pasture with his booty clattering. Some have heard the hammering of nails and the feeble pounding of a man buried beneath the pleasant green grass.

You see that spot up ahead? That's where they found Emma Bell, or so it's told. She was soaked from rain, staring off toward the swamp. She had taken one of those old Indian arrowheads and cut her own throat. Sharp medicine, they called it.

The Second Parsonage

Secrets are safe with me. I'll take them to my grave, my heart a cache of kisses and curses. It has everything to do with my nature . . . words whispered in confidence sink into me like stones in a dark pond. That is my one exceptional attribute, my singular gift.

I am a schoolmaster by trade, and in the spring of 1830 I attained that position in the town of Whitney, following my predecessor, a Mr. Grimes, who, cooked thoroughly by fever, was whisked off to oblivion. Whitney was a small farming town high in the hilly woods of north-central Massachusetts. It was a humble, if forgettable place, with more fields than houses and more crows than fields. Dusky brooks gulped and tangled in the enclosing pines and an arthritic old tannery pitched above the murkiest pond ever to tempt geese.

The schoolhouse was perfunctory at best—built before the invention of rain, there was no part of the floor that did not creak when stepped upon. Still, I went about my duties to the best of my ability and my students, for the most part, were an agreeable lot.

I have not mentioned that it was May. The days were growing longer, the woods greener, and the sunsets blushed like a bride. One fine day a student, the son of a farmer, approached my desk at the end of lessons. Squinting between freckles, his clothing seemingly made of dirt, this boy stood expectantly, creaking the floor, cracking his knuckles like beech pods.

"Yes?" I said.

"I have a secret," the lad intoned softly.

"Do you, now?"

The boy nodded. "Would you like to hear it?"

Ironically enough, for a teacher, I never had learned *my* lesson. Secrets are like lions . . . let them sleep! "Certainly," I said.

The boy creaked closer and I bent to receive his whisper.

"Do you know the house on the other side of the pond?"

"The old parsonage?" I asked.

"It's the second one—the first burnt down."

"At any rate," I said, "I know the house of which you speak."

"A dead man lives there."

I rented a room in the house of William Higley, the undertaker. It was the best that my schoolmaster's wage could provide, which is not to say that my situation was disagreeable. The landlord was not fond of conversation, and was thus suited to his profession, seeming to prefer the company of his charges above that of his loquacious wife. Upon meeting a person for the first time, Higley looked them up and down as if sizing for a coffin. I suppose it was an instinct.

One evening, dining with the couple, I ventured a question. While impervious to common temptations, and while a team of oxen could not drag from me a secret once interred, my curiosity had been incited by my young student.

"Would the old parsonage beyond the pond be yet inhabited?"

The question had a curious effect on the Higleys; the wife fell into an uncharacteristic silence and the undertaker actually spoke.

"One would hardly think so, to look upon the place," the man said soberly.

I waited as if more were forthcoming, but nothing further was volunteered. The three of us simply sat there, chewing away like cows. I was intrigued, nonetheless, for Higley's remark implied that the parsonage was indeed occupied.

Later, in my chamber, I invested a measure of time to conjure a pretense with which to pay visit to the old house. *"A dead man lives there,"* the child had said. While absurd—a "dead" man can not *live* anywhere—it was enough to intrigue my ample imagination. Whatever made that boy think such a thing? Perhaps the resident was a sickly sort, or of a particularly unpleasant aspect to gaze upon, disfigured in some way, or bearing an unwholesome pallor. I would find out soon enough, for I was determined to call upon the old parsonage the very next day.

I decided that I would borrow one of Mr. Higley's horses, go to the place in question, and present myself as a concerned neighbor who, having found the beast straying along the road, was seeking to find its owner. It seemed a believable enough fabrication and, with any luck, heaven would forgive my dishonesty.

A good spring rain pummeled the schoolhouse the next morning. Muffled above, it had a sound like pigeons complaining under water. The floor creaked, the roof leaked, and my pupils sat yawning through their lessons. The storminess cleared off in time for my investigation, however, and I went back to Higley's stable to fetch a horse. Higley had agreed to allow me use of the beast for the afternoon. Despite my vagueness, he did not appear curious as to my reason for wanting the creature.

Not terribly fond of riding on the backs of large quadrupeds, most certainly without a saddle, I walked the black gelding the distance to the parsonage, passing Whitney's third such structure on my way. The town's first parsonage had burned down in the middle of the last century and was replaced by that house to which I was headed. Not altogether familiar with the particulars of the town's history, I knew only that the third parsonage was erected when the minister's purse entitled him and his brood to finer environs. I'd heard it said that the minister's wife insisted on something other than the drafty behemoth there by Fitch's Pond.

It was a fine afternoon; the sky was blue but for some puffy white clouds like corpulent nudes. I came within view of the pond, which was a sizeable study so far as those things go. The tannery stood on one side, and the old parsonage on the other. Each was built before the Revolution, and both struck me as precarious, balancing there. I imagined that a slight tug from gravity would land them both in the pond, where mysterious currents might shape their timbers into an ark to whisk the townsfolk straight down the Styx.

I was becoming something of a master liar by this time, having fended off several inquisitive townsfolk between the Higley property and the pond. It has been my experience that people in small towns have an insatiable hunger after their neighbors' business. I gave each a different tale—while trying not to smirk—and, for the most part, they seemed placated by my creations. The poor animal suffered a cramp that I was walking out, I told one. The beast escaped and I had tracked it down, I told another. And then there was my prize offering: I told the prying Mrs. Fuller that I was a remarkable athlete and had been racing the horse for sport. I won, of course, I told her. She turned an interesting shade of red and hurried about her way.

The nudes in the sky were transforming, stretching grotesquely as they dissolved into the blue. The parsonage stood imposingly, the way it had for some eighty-odd years, as I and my plodding companion approached. Upon gazing up at the place I was reminded of the undertaker's words: the appearance of the house suggested that it was uninhabited, such was its sad state. I also fell in sympathy with the minister's wife's desire for a more appealing dwelling.

Colonists had built the thing, and it was not unlike the other shelters of that time, a two-story structure with a low-pitched roof and simple frame. This particular rendition boasted twin chimneys close to the gable ends, and a formal entry with pairs of windows situated symmetrically to either side. Five windows looked down from the façade's second floor. A simple ell jutted out from the back of the main building.

It had not been all that many years since the minister and his family moved on to their more stylish abode, and yet it seemed this place had been in the teeth of the elements for an exorbitant amount of time. The thin clapboards were dark with mildew, their previous paint color entirely indistinguishable. The roof was missing shingles and some of the window panes were webbed with cracks. Even the cartway, little more than a suggestion of ruts leading to the forgotten dooryard garden, was lost to invasive grass. I found the moldering water barrel crouched at the left front corner particularly unsettling—like a drowned mouth full of dark rain. The few remnants of fence pickets might have been bones poking up from eroded graves.

I will admit that a degree of hesitancy came over me, but I have the curiosity of a cat, and thus proceeded. I tethered the horse to a piece of fence and walked up to the old paneled door and gave it a knock. No response was forthcoming. Even my louder thumps were in vain—no sign of life came from the place. I looked to the windows, but they were awash in the glare of slanting afternoon light, and I could distinguish nothing but my own squinting reflection.

"Hullo!" I called, and still there was no response.

Half-relieved, I turned, walked to the crippled fence, and gathered the horse's lead. I headed back for the village proper, my interest in mystery tempered with an inexplicable sense of dread. It would be months before I was to return to this place.

Later, in my apartment, my courage restored by the safety of distance, I chastised myself for not persisting. I might have seen into the shady rear windows, or placed successful raps on a side door, had I tried. At any rate . . .

The seasons went about their course and I learned little more about the second parsonage and its alleged occupant in the months that followed that first excursion. As indicated, my fascination had lost some of its vigor, although I did make a number of half-hearted inquiries. Those native to Whitney, while usually swift to whisper about this or that neighbor, had little to say on the matter.

I took it that the old house's occupant was as solitary as a man could be, venturing from his abode only in the still of wintry nights, according to one young fellow from the cider mill. But how could that be so? How might one conduct the business of his life in so restricted a manner? Others told me that his name was Swan, and that little to nothing was known of his history, only that he had arrived one bleak November day, purchased the deserted house by the pond, and filled it with cartloads of wooden crates (or their contents). He had no friends, no kin, no contact whatsoever with the others in that locality.

Every teacher has his or her favorite student, or so I would attest. I was particularly fond of Almira Goodridge, the cooper's daughter, who, at ten years of age, was smarter than all of my boy wards combined. She was quick to laugh, quick to learn, and drawn to wildflowers like a bee. She was all that youth ought to be, as innocent and full of promise as a May morning.

One day in autumn, when the harvest kept most of my students away from the schoolroom, blond-haired Almira was bounding down the stairs in her house, singing. She had the voice of an angel and was very fond of music and the sound of birds. For one unfortunate moment, she lost her footing and went tumbling down the stairs. She broke her neck and died on the spot. Her song, only partly sung, silenced in an instant.

It was in the parlor of the Goodridge house, with rain weeping on the outside and relations of the dead child weeping on the inside, that I began to think again upon the sad, old parsonage. The girl lay in her box as if merely sleeping, her hair as gold as it had ever been, as gold as August fields, or birch leaves in autumn, gold as honey bees and sunflowers. But her hair would grow no longer, and the cooper's house would never again be filled with her clear singing, or the mirthful bursting of her laughter. As I stood there looking down at her, I felt the pull of that dreary building by Fitch's Pond. I might as well have been a leaf dropped from a tree and taken by the wind through no act of will. I would return to that place the following day.

It was an afternoon in October; the sunlight was warm, the air was cool, and the month, grown tired of its colors, had shed the better part of them, content to reveal gnarled trees and expanded views. Distant farms appeared suddenly from the landscape, exhausted fields and all, and pastures—still green enough for cows—nearly glowed in the late-day light, shadow-textured by their own unevenness.

Unaccountably determined, I went straightaway to the decaying parsonage without so much as candle or armament. It stood as it had before, a solemn thing there by the dark pond. No smoke rose from the chimneys, though the day grew chill; no glow came from the windows, though the light was failing. I passed the few remaining fence pickets, or what I could see of them through the tall grass, and found myself at the front door. I had nothing to say, no rational purpose, and yet there I was, fixed to gain entry.

I knocked. There came no answer. I knocked again and still there was no response. I tried the door and found it unlocked. It screeched like a cat as it opened.

"Hullo. . . ?"

My voice echoed in the dim center passage and rose hollowly up the stairs. While a trespasser, I was not entirely without manners, and thus closed the door through which I had stolen. It was as gloomy inside as I had imagined, lacking any décor—no pictures, nor lamps or sconces on the walls. There was a door to my left and a door to my right, these no doubt leading to front parlors. For no reason in particular, I chose the left.

Houses often make an impression on my sense of smell before anything else, and such was the case here. I was taken by a stifling mustiness which, if interpreted visually, would best have been conjured in shades of sepia. The room was no longer a parlor in the traditional sense, though the structural elements remained intact; the fireplace wall was handsomely paneled, the wainscoting was in good repair, and the floor was composed of the widest planks I had seen in some time. As for chairs and tables, or any of the comforts one might expect, there were none.

What there were, however, were *books!* A maze of dusty books in crazy stacks as tall as a man. The dull, leather-bound tomes covered much of the floor, allowing only narrow paths between them. How very strange, I thought. It offended my sensibilities in one sense, for I am fond of an orderly library—certainly these volumes deserved better treatment than this. I lingered only a moment, returned to the entryway, and tried the opposite door.

This room was the same as the last—stacked books, webs, and nothing more—no furnishings whatsoever. The old parsonage, I soon found, was full of books front to back, even the kitchen (stripped of tables, and containing not a single pot or scrap of food) and the abandoned servant quarters in the ell. Whoever this Swan fellow was, whether dead or alive, he was undoubtedly an eccentric creature.

I made my way up the front staircase, pausing at the top to listen for signs of occupation. Suddenly I was less than keen on the prospect of encountering the man who was said to dwell in the place. The townsfolk, I suddenly told myself, must surely be mistaken in believing that anyone actually lived in the house. That would explain the infrequent sightings of Swan—he was obviously using the house to store books, not to dwell in. This theory was bolstered by the fact that even the bedchambers contained only more books. If Swan lived there, then where did he sleep?

It was not until this point, in an upper apartment overlooking the dark sprawl of Fitch's Pond, that I actually examined one of the books. It was a heavy thing, bound in pebbly leather the color of cooked liver. A simple "L" was carved into the binding. Inside I found only names and dates, inked in by the same steady hand. It seemed to be a ledger of sorts, with the names alphabetically arranged. But what was curious was that these birth and death records, as they seemed to be, ranged far into the future, with listings like this: *James Martin Leighton, 19th of March, 1956 – 2nd of December, 2011.*

I tried to think of some acquaintance whose name began with an L and recalled a certain Joseph Lewis, a tinsmith from my hometown of Eastborough. He had departed this mortal realm some two years previous. I flipped though the pages and found many a Lewis, at last locating his name in particular, and sure enough, the birth date and death listing reflected the truth as I knew it to be. Not only was Joseph represented, but his entire family past and present, and, from the looks of it, every Lewis ever to walk the earth.

I was so intrigued by this new mystery, so busy investigating more of the books, that I forgot all about worrying over Mr. Swan. I made my way from room to room as the declining October light softened the windows, and the skinny aisles between the stacks filled with shadow. I was now looking up specific people.

In a pile of books marked with a "G," I found Almira Goodridge: *10th of August, 1820 – 16th of October, 1830*. The information was correct. There were entries dating to the centuries before Christ, and to those yet to be. There were names from every language, from every country, the names of every person who had ever lived, and all those to come. All of humankind was logged in those books in those darkening old rooms, and I was privy to the information.

In another upstairs bedroom, I looked up my own family. My deceased parents' dates were indeed accurate, and I found my three living sisters listed as well. It appeared as if they would enjoy lengthy enough lives, if the book were to be believed. It was clear to me that the books revealed *when* a person would die and, curious cat that I am, I had to know . . .

I was tracing my finger down the yellowed page to find my own name when the door behind me groaned open. I turned with a shudder as a tall figure shuffled into the room. Swan stopped and regarded me across the precariously heaped books. The chamber had become rather dark, so he was largely obscured in shadow. I could tell little about his dress—it might have been a robe of sorts—but it was plain that a great beard the color of frost was wound about his head like bandages, or a bee skep. Of his features only the eyes were to be seen, and just barely at that, small and pale, peering though a gap in the coil.

I was frozen in place with the book still open in my hands, hovering before me as I stared. The old man—God, or Death, or something we haven't even a name for—raised a thin hand and pointed at the book. I nodded, swallowed, and dropped my eyes to the page. I looked to where my finger rested, alongside my own name, and I read the dates.

Looking back up, a trembling little smile came to my lips. According to the entry, I would live a very long life. The wrapped head nodded and the old man raised a finger to where his mouth would be and said, "Ssshhhh," and then gestured toward the door.

I cannot tell you the relief I felt, the flood of exhilaration, as I made my way through the dusty structure and out into the chill dusk. I had never felt so alive in all my years. Life, for all its dark ponds and sad old buildings, is a thing of beauty! I began to sing—a song of my own making, a song to the fleeting copper sunset—as I headed back toward the village proper. You, too, should sing while you can, for we are all listed in the books there in the second parsonage, and I could tell you the date of *your* death, but it's a secret.